1369
WAT

KT-399-601

MIDWIFERY

ADULTS LEARNING

ADULTS LEARNING

THIRD EDITION

Jenny Rogers

MEDICAL LIBRARY
WATFORD POSTGRADUATE
MEDICAL CENTRE
WATFORD GENERAL HOSPITAL
VICARAGE ROAD
WATFORD WD1 8HB

OPEN UNIVERSITY PRESS
Milton Keynes · Philadelphia

Open University Press
Celtic Court
22 Ballmoor
Buckingham MK18 1XW

and
1900 Frost Road, Suite 101,
Bristol, PA 19007, USA

First Published 1971
Reprinted in this edition 1977
First published in second edition 1977
Reprinted 1979, 1984, 1986, 1988
First published in this edition 1989
Reprinted 1992

Copyright © Jenny Rogers 1971, 1977, 1989

All rights reserved. No part of this publication may be reproduced, stored in a retrieval system or transmitted in any form or by any means, without written permission from the publisher.

British Library Cataloguing in Publication Data
Rogers, Jenny, *1939–*
1. Adults learning – 3rd ed. Great Britain. Adult education. Teaching methods
I. Title
374'.02

ISBN 0-335-09215-2

Library of Congress Cataloging in Publication number available

Typeset by Rowland Phototypesetting Ltd
Bury St Edmunds, Suffolk
Printed in Great Britain by The Bath Press Ltd, Avon

Contents

	Introduction	1
1	Being a learner	9
2	What makes adults want to learn?	27
3	How do adults learn?	39
4	Giving feedback	57
5	Understanding your group	69
6	Teaching mixed ability groups	91
7	The first session	105
8	Lectures and demonstrations	118
9	Case studies, role play, simulation and games	126
10	Tutoring open learners	143
11	Projects	158
12	Discussion	174
	Bibliography	195
	Index	197

Introduction

This book is addressed to people who teach adults wherever adults are learning: for instance, in business and industry, in 'leisure' classes, on government training schemes, in management education or perhaps through 'open' learning.

If you teach adults in these situations you may be unaware that you have anything in common with other tutors in different environments. Your organization may be jealous of its own status and special interests. Also, to some tutors, the content of what is to be taught may seem more important than looking at whether there are methods which are generally appropriate to all adult learning.

It is true that there are many ways in which the subject itself dictates the methods, but this book does not and could not go into the special problems of teaching adults supervisory management skills or philosophy or modern Greek. Instead, I have tried to suggest that the art of teaching adults is a broadly-based and flexible one, whose principles can be applied and adapted to a wide variety of situations.

I have not attempted to offer any easy, infallible guides to 'good' teaching. Teaching and learning are such infinitely variable processes that you and your learners will always have particular needs which only you and they can interpret. The suggestions made about methods, approaches and materials are meant to outline a range of possibilities from which you and your class can choose, rather than a set of rules to which you must always adhere.

The first chapters are about adult students: who they are, what brings them to classes, how they feel in a classroom, how they learn most easily, how they behave in groups, and with what sorts of tutors and teaching methods they are likely to feel happiest.

The second half of the book is about practicalities: the advantages and disadvantages of particular teaching strategies such as role play, discussion, or projects. These chapters also deal with the problems of planning resources, of finding ways of giving individual attention to students in classes of widely varying ability, and of creating active, lively methods of learning.

One of the difficulties about teaching is its isolation. Tutors only rarely see, or are seen by, other tutors in action. We are largely protected by the awe, politeness or simply the indifference of our classes from knowing how learners really assess our teaching. As one class member, quoted later in the book, said of a hard-working, conscientious but incompetent teacher: 'It was less trouble to leave the class than to explain to him that he was going about fifty times too fast.'

This is why, throughout the book, I have illustrated certain points by direct quotation, where tutors and students of varied backgrounds and subjects describe their classroom experiences and speak for themselves. The quotes were solicited in an entirely *ad hoc* and non-sociological manner. Many friends and professional acquaintances generously wrote pieces themselves, and also collected an enormous amount of material for me from their students and colleagues. Most of these accounts were lengthy and absorbing, and it has only been possible to quote a few paragraphs from them. Others were written as notes and have been reconstructed as accurately as possible in continuous form. Some are verbatim descriptions taken down on tape or by hand. Since most of them are frank and some of them blunt, identifying details have been changed where necessary.

This book was first published in 1971, and amended in 1973. In 1977 I used the fidgety, enforced leisure brought about by the raised blood pressure of my second pregnancy to prepare a new edition. Now, twelve years later, the child of that pregnancy is entering adolescence, and the book again needs updating.

It is a hard task to write a book about teaching without sounding prescriptive or saintly – or possibly both. In the first two editions I did not attempt to explain how and why I had come to write it, perhaps because the experience was still too recent or perhaps because I was sensitive to the possible accusation that I was too young and inexperienced to be writing a book of 'advice' at all.

The book came out of two strands of experience: my own in the classroom and my early years with the BBC. My own direct classroom teaching was in Colleges of Further Education where teaching adults became an important part of a job which I had originally thought was going to be exclusively about the education of sixteen- to nineteen-year-olds. To survive and to learn your craft in this environment your wits had to be sharp and your sense of humour well to the fore. As the youngest person in my 'adult' O-level English class, I was the teacher, but without any of the natural authority that age and experience conferred: no wonder that I often felt I was engaged in a role play rather than the real thing. In the daytime I found myself in some equally tricky situations, for instance with a class of seventeen-year-olds to whom I was teaching Economics, a subject I loathed and where the students had the advantage of having studied for a year longer than I. Their merciless teasing taught me a great deal about the need to love the subject you teach and the absolute necessity for burning to communicate your pleasure in it.

Where the adult students were polite and reticent, the sparky young people I taught in the daytime never hesitated to give me candid feedback on my performance: 'Bit boring today, Miss – too much theory', or 'I liked that bit where we read the play instead of you talking'. They had gloriously direct ways of teaching teachers humbling lessons. One day, a favourite group of eighteen-year-olds was mysteriously late coming into the classroom. Only the two class swots sat there politely exchanging desultory conversation with me in a silent classroom. After ten minutes of this, I enquired again what on earth they thought had happened to the others. Apparently as baffled as I, they just shook their heads dumbly. Seconds later, the door of the classroom cupboard burst open and out tumbled the other fifteen members of my class, gasping for air and beaming. 'We know you especially like discussing things with Tom and Pauline, so we thought we'd play a little trick.' Only eighteen-year-olds could so ruthlessly and innocently rub home this important lesson: like many teachers, I was talking to the 'good students' far too much. They were telling me that they would all like a share.

In effect my younger students trained me and I diligently and gratefully applied what I was learning to the adult classes where exactly the same forces were at work, but much more discreetly. After all, the adults did not have to be there: if the class was disagreeable, they could simply stop coming. The overriding impact of this experience amounted to one simple message: in teaching, the customer, not the subject, comes first and is always right, and the customer is the learner.

However valuable this experience was, it was considerably sharpened by my first job at the BBC. If only every tutor could, as I did, sit anonymously in other people's classrooms. The 'mistakes' that we all fudge in our own teaching become burningly obvious when looking at someone else making them. This privilege came my way because, as a new young BBC Education Officer, I was able to visit all kinds of adult classes as part of my remit: to advise the BBC on the quality of its adult education programmes and to point up directions they might pursue in the future.

Since nobody in adult and further education really believed that the BBC knew anything at all about teaching, I was welcomed everywhere. 'It's only some girl from the BBC', I overheard one principal explaining to one of his tutors. 'She just wants to sit in the back – it's not like having an inspector here.' So, as an honorary invisible woman, I saw adult teaching of all types – probably several hundred classes eventually – in the raw. I was witness to some fine teaching in the most acutely uncomfortable circumstances – I often came home with cramp in my calves and pain in the knees after sitting for two hours at an infant's desk – but exhilarated by the quality and quantity of the learning I had observed. I saw bold and innovative teaching that was years ahead of its time – especially in trade union and management education. But equally, and perhaps more often, I saw tutors struggling because no one had apparently even attempted to show them solutions to the common problems of all teaching: how to motivate, how to sustain interest, how to help people learn. The ever-shifting population of part-timers and the rampant neglect of the adult education sector by virtually all Local Education Authorities made such problems acute.

One piece of good fortune fuelled my desire to pass on to others what I felt I now knew. In my first year at the BBC I was asked to help evaluate a series called *Teaching Adults*, produced by two BBC stalwarts, Roger Owen and Tony Cash. The series became a classic and my work on it took me right to the heart of the debate on adult learning by introducing me to many of the best brains in the business. Some of them contributed to the book I edited for BBC Publications, *Teaching on Equal Terms*, but working on this project made me even keener to write a book entirely my own, hence *Adults Learning*.

Working on this new edition has brought home to me how much adult education has changed in the nearly twenty years that have passed since I began writing the original book. Many of the debates that were then vibrant have died. The fruitless wrangling over whether television is friend or foe has been replaced by the wearier recognition that it is a bit of both. The great hopes, relic of the 1930s, that adult education would be the powerhouse of a working-class revolution have proved false: trade unionism is diminishing as a 'movement', whether from self-inflicted wounds, from general prosperity or from Conservative assaults, and with it the desire for 'working-class self-help' which now seems curiously irrelevant to the meaner spirit of our times.

Most significantly of all, the passionate discussion about whether 'vocational' can be as 'good' as 'liberal' (or non-vocational) education seems dead indeed. The question now seems to be whether non-vocational education can have any value. That this question could even be framed would have seemed preposterous in the 1960s.

This change has come about with the end of full employment, the oil crisis of the early 1970s, and the inflation and then recession that followed. Computerization has brought an end to hundreds of thousands of jobs. Unskilled jobs will never again be easy to find. In many parts of the country there is likely to be a high unemployment rate for many years to come. 'The problem of leisure', a favourite 1960s theme in adult education, which assumed that work would diminish all round, leaving a bored and prosperous population suckers for the Evening Institutes, now has a sour note. There *is* a 'problem' of leisure, certainly, but the problem is the unwanted leisure of unemployed people who have no money to spend on it, while those of us in paid employment work even longer hours for higher-than-ever salaries. When I was recently bemoaning my all-too-frequent twelve-hour days with a management consultant acquaintance, he stared at me stonily and informed me flatly that all professional people worth their salt now work twelve-hour days – or longer. Professional people may have little leisure, but they are very much in the market for education – as long as you call it 'training' and relate it to their jobs.

With these trends a powerful new adult education agency entered the field in the early 1970s: the Manpower Services Commission (MSC), briefly redubbed the Training Commission, now the Training Agency. Where adult educationists had for years wrung their hands helplessly about the 'need' for education, the MSC swept in with its billion-pound budgets and the political embarrassment of high unemployment figures. With hundreds of thousands of training places a year, many of them for just those reluctant learners apparently rejected by the schools, the MSC grew to rival and perhaps to outstrip in political muscle the politer kind of 'pure' education traditionally espoused by the Department of Education and Science. It has even reached successfully into schools and has become a major client of the post-sixteen colleges.

Rumour has it that these great Departments are not friends. The boast that the MSC did tomorrow what the DES set a Royal Commission to report on in three years' time was met by the counter-accusation that MSC/Training Agency schemes were fly-by-nights, originated, changed and suddenly abandoned at political whim.

Perhaps those mutual recriminations are less important than the underlying trends which go much deeper than Civil Service rivalry. For every day that the average British working adult spends in training, the average German spends ten. The success of the Japanese economy is at least partly attributable to the importance the Japanese give to education, training and retraining. The shift from 'adult education' to 'continuing education' is more than just a modish piece of labelling. 'Adult education' unfortunately never meant 'the education of all adults', but something that might, if you were lucky, patch up a few holes in your previous education. 'Continuing education' at least implies that education is not a process which stops with the end of full-time education, but which is rather something that all people are likely to need at regular intervals during their lives. In my own career I have so far had five distinctly different jobs and for each of them I have needed (but not always had access to) major chunks of training and education as well as a lot of modest pieces of infilling such as how to operate a word processor or video-editing machine. And this is leaving aside any personal obsessions such as learning in my mid-thirties to play badminton and to speak Italian, or in my mid-forties to replace a near-doggy-paddle with a proper front crawl in the swimming pool.

The rapid outmoding of previous knowledge is behind the 'continuing professional development' which will soon be a feature, sometimes mandatory, of many of the major professions. Other shocks are on the way. The National Council for Vocational Qualifications (NCVQ) will have profound effects on training and ultimately on all education. Gone will be any element of time-serving and 'knowledge for its own sake'. Can people prove that they have the skills to do the job? If so, then no matter how or where they have learnt, they are entitled to the qualification. And the qualification should be linked only to the competencies you need to do the job: no more and no less. Do junior sales people really need to know the theory of retail distribution in the United Kingdom, or do they actually just need to know how to diagnose a customer's needs quickly in order to make the sale? If the latter, then, it is argued, there is absolutely no point in learning the theory and every point in focusing on practical rehearsals for the real thing.

NCVQ is already having a considerable effect on vocational training by obliging employers, examining bodies and professional associations to look closely at what skills are actually needed to do the job. This, in its turn, is bound to mean a far sharper-eyed look at the quality of training and the professionalism of the trainers themselves.

One other tremendous change is under way. This is a demographic crisis which will have far-reaching effects. By the mid-1990s, the number of eighteen-year-olds will have fallen to its lowest point for many years. Many professions – for instance accountancy and nursing – will be absolutely unable to fill all their vacant places by traditional means. They will need to look instead at the possibility of recruiting mature adults. It is unlikely that such people will be attracted by or would tolerate the style of much present training with its encouragement, in many cases, of child-like dependence on traditional classroom teaching.

In spite of all this emphasis on vocational learning, the traditional adult education sector has survived and grown. Alert to the possibility that it was only catering for the already privileged, there is now a thriving sector dealing with 'special needs' – a euphemism for the handicapped and disabled and for people who are 'socially disadvantaged'. Craft classes are as full as they ever were; yoga and keep fit still boom. At the other end of the spectrum, the enormous success of the Open University shows that 'knowledge for its own sake' and 'proving something to yourself' still have the power to draw. Even here, though, there are signs of our times. The most astonishing growth area of the Open University over the last few years has been its Open Business School: a management training organization whose students' fees are almost always paid by employers.

My own former employer, The Open College, has also set its

sights firmly on the vocational market. Its sponsoring parent was the MSC, so perhaps it is not surprising that it is *not* to be 'the People's College', or 'the cloth-cap Open University' that many people imagined or hoped. Instead, everything that is done has to be linked to vocational training, and the qualifications offered must ultimately fit within the NCVQ framework.

The growth of 'open' learning is in itself one of the significant success stories of the last twenty years. Whether 'distance learning', 'flexistudy', 'correspondence education', 'Open Tech Programme', Open University, or 'directed private study', the trend is notable. Perhaps it is not surprising: the main demand for training and further learning comes from twenty- to thirty-five-year-olds, the very people most likely to be deeply and perhaps quite happily enmeshed in nest-building. Face-to-face teaching will always need the guaranteed numbers and set times which busy adults often simply cannot manage. Working 'own pace, own place' thus has much appeal, and so, too, does the emphasis on being in control of your own learning which the best open learning will always give to a student.

This, then, is the kind of scene I have had in mind while preparing this substantially rewritten new edition. In writing the first edition I tried to write the kind of book I wished someone had given me when I was new to teaching and approached each class with a mixture of terror and elation. My mental identikit portrait of my typical reader was a new part-timer at an Adult Education Centre or a supervisor in industry told on Friday that from Monday he was to be the training officer. To these two typical readers I now add an imagined gallery of others: a nurse tutor in a nursing school who knows she soon faces a group of 'returners to nursing' for the first time; an experienced classroom teacher of young adolescents who now finds she is taking on a group of allegedly 'unruly' YTS trainees; a polytechnic Business Studies lecturer drawn into teaching a Training Agency short course for people starting up their own business; an Open College or Open University tutor with little recent experience of teaching adults but a good deal of knowledge and love of the subjects he is tutoring.

I remain committed to my original vision that the principles of teaching adults are the same whatever the setting, the types of learner or the subject. The effective teacher of adults has only one motto, and that is: 'Learners first'. How you might put that motto into practice is what the rest of this book is about.

1

Being a learner

When I was a very new teacher, I was most unwisely set to do my duty on enrolment night at the college where I was working. One of my first customers wanted to enrol for Beginners' Italian. I asked her, as I had been told to do, whether she knew any Italian and if so how much. She confided cheerfully that this would be her third year in the Italian beginners' class. She particularly liked the tutor, but it was not just that. She still did not feel confident enough of her Italian to progress to the second year. She was afraid of finding it all too much, of looking silly, and that was why she wanted the comfort and familiarity of Beginners' Italian all over again.

This was my first encounter with one of the most striking features of adult students: their anxiety that they might be making themselves look foolish, or that they might be exposing themselves to failure. This sort of anxiety is not confined to the students who come to 'recreational' classes, nor is it confined to the unsophisticated and poorly educated. On the contrary, it seems to apply right across the range of adult students. Out of dozens of pieces of writing I have collected from teachers and students on this theme, I have chosen the illustrations below, not for any particular originality or eccentricity, but because they seem to reflect the typical anxieties of adult students.

> For months before this training course started I used to dream about looking stupid on it, and of making it look that I was incapable of doing the job. I was astonished at myself – a Cambridge 'first' and all – being so worried about going 'back to school', but I used to think to myself, oh well, in another three months, two months, one month, it'll all be over.

> We were told we were going to have a 'free discussion' and that we were all going to be expected to speak. That was all right for those who'd been at school more recently than me, but I'd been a mere housewife only a week before and I made up my mind on the spot that wild horses wouldn't drag any 'discussion' out of me. I knew I'd say something silly.

> The whole point of drama is that you step out of yourself, and this is what I wanted to achieve, but the self-consciousness which I hoped to lose when I joined the class in the first place was a most severe barrier to shedding it! Every time it came to my turn I'd get butterflies in my stomach, though I tried desperately to conceal my nervousness. Everyone in the class was a colleague of mine and I did not like them to see how afraid I was. Also, never having done any acting before, I knew my performances would be bad and I did not like doing anything badly, particularly in front of people who knew me as an efficient person in other ways.

> I've enrolled this year for cookery – but demonstrations only. I don't want to do anything myself. I had enough of that last year – made hundreds of mistakes which was a laugh for everybody else, not much fun for me.

> We all know the difficulties of obtaining written essays from students. I believe the reason is that a student who knows he has impressed you in class is afraid you will 'see through' him if he puts anything down on paper. There is often a deep-seated sense of inadequacy in my students, even though many of them are successful professional men and women. They associate written work with tests, marks and examinations, and therefore with potential failure.

Research has even produced physical proof of this sort of fear and anxiety in adult learners. One experiment showed that if blood tests are taken from adults before, during and after engaging in a piece of learning, there is a rise in the level of free fatty acids in the blood as the learning proceeds, a rise which becomes more noticeable and persists longer the older the learner is. Free fatty acids are a good measure of emotional stress, and a high level can in itself prevent people learning efficiently. Thus the anxiety of the adult who is afraid of looking silly can itself be the cause of a poor performance and can confirm the learner's worst fears. It will be particularly noticeable where a skill like weaving, driving or embroidery is being taught, because fumbling or trembling fingers and the ineptitudes they cause will then be obvious. Experienced tutors in more cerebral subjects will be equally familiar with the blushing, the tense, worried looks and hesitant voices of students who are not altogether confident of their own abilities and judgements.

There are exceptions, of course. Younger students, especially those who have just left school or college, may experience no worries at all because they feel they are in a familiar environment. One young woman, who had graduated in sociology only a few months before, started her description of her experiences in a literature and philosophy class in the following crisp and confident way:

> I was really looking forward to joining the class and learning a new subject. I did not feel at all nervous as I have walked into many a lecture hall, and felt fully capable of tackling anything the lecturer was prepared to give me.

This type of student does not expect to find the work difficult and has evidently regarded education as an entirely enjoyable and stimulating experience. Youth and vitality are on her side, and with a degree newly in her pocket she feels she has no cause to be worried by anything in her philosophy class, because it is merely an informal continuation of a process in which she has already proved herself.

There are plenty of other students who will not suffer from feelings of nervousness and tension – for instance, those women who have been going to the same dressmaking class, with the same tutor for many years (some classes have been known to continue for sixteen); the people who go to courses where 'teaching' goes on but not necessarily learning (public lectures an hour long followed by five or ten minutes' discussion would be an extreme example). Any course where there is no testing of any kind will have relaxed students; but then, very frequently in such cases, although there is no anxiety, there is no learning either, because there is no wish for change in either students or teacher.

Obviously, in voluntary adult education at least, anxiety will not be the predominant emotion in students' minds, otherwise they would never enrol at all. Interest and lively curiosity will be much stronger in the majority of students. You can also bear in mind that nervousness can be fairly easily allayed and that, although it may indeed be desirable always to keep the atmosphere at least alert, extreme tension in your students should not be a major problem after the first few classes. In a well-integrated group your role in reducing anxiety will become less central as your students realize that the work is within their grasp.

Nevertheless, research and common observation show that some tension is always likely to be present when adults are learning, and that this tension is likely to increase and to be more of a handicap the older the students are and the greater the pressure that is put upon them. It is understandable that men and women on industrial training courses should be concerned about their performance, as very frequently their jobs or promotions depend on how well they do, whether this is retraining for the middle-aged or the initial training now given to most new recruits.

At first sight it may seem surprising that learners who are volunteers should feel such worries, especially as surveys show that the major clientele for further education is precisely that part of the population which is most 'experienced' educationally and that might be expected therefore to be least frightened of returning to the classroom. Perhaps the worries of many adults about returning to the classroom have a lot to do with the widely held idea that education is a process which only concerns children. The hopeful concept of 'lifelong' or 'continuing education' where broadly-based education would come to play a major role throughout everyone's life is still very far from being a generally accepted idea.

As adults we are, after all, people who have come to acquire the status of maturity in our own and other people's eyes as husbands, wives, parents, friends, employers or employees. Perhaps this status and self-esteem are less robust than they appear, and are easily threatened when we are put back in what may appear to be the subordinate position of the learner.

Psychologists like Carl Rogers, searching for a more thoroughgoing theoretical basis for this anxiety, have found it in theories which point out what potential conflict is involved when an adult comes to a class (particularly perhaps in academic subjects or any areas where values are involved). The conflict is that as adults we already have certain well-developed ideas about life along with our own systems of ideas and beliefs. To admit that we need to learn something new is to admit that there is something wrong with our present system. Many people, although they may dimly perceive their need for new knowledge, may feel so threatened by the challenge to their previous beliefs that they are unable to learn. For instance, a young mother may realize that she needs to learn more about her child's development and may enrol for a class in child psychology. Once there, she may filter out or refuse to understand anything the teacher and the rest of the class say with which she does not agree, as this might be tantamount to admitting that her present way of looking after her child is mistaken and that she has been in some way a 'bad' mother.

This may be why adult students often take refuge in the unconscious subterfuge that what we are learning is really meant for somebody else. I remember a refresher course organized for the whole staff of a college where I was teaching, which everyone was pressed, perhaps clumsily and unwisely, to attend. It was a stimulating and well-planned short course of lectures and discussions conducted by a retired college of further education lecturer. We all attended with much show of grumbling reluctance. Even though most of us clearly enjoyed ourselves at the time and learnt a certain amount, it would have been impossible to find a single member of the full-time staff willing to admit that the lectures were aimed at us. No, they were meant for 'inexperienced', 'very young' or 'part-time' teachers. To have admitted that we needed instruction would have aimed too sharp a blow at our ideas of ourselves as already professionally competent teachers. The unknowable element here is whether we would have learnt more had the course been more tactfully presented to us as an occasion where we could usefully discuss common problems (which it most valuably was) rather than as something which implied we were deficient in some respect (as perhaps we were). As it was, there were, every week, one or two people who made a point of shutting their eyes throughout the whole ninety-minute session or who prepared lesson notes and wrote letters, and a few more who conspicuously absented themselves at the last minute with much elaborate apologizing to the lecturer.

The lessons for tutors seem to be that courses must clearly be planned to help adults preserve at least part of their 'self-image'. The value of the students' previous experience must be generously acknowledged and used as a basis for building up more experience and gaining further knowledge. This will be particularly important on industrial or professional courses, where some element of external compulsion may operate.

Adult learners' feelings are going to differ very much from one individual to another and from one situation to another. Mature women students in their first year of a teacher-training course are likely to be more humble and more openly anxious than a group of experienced managers on a short management training course. Adult 'non-readers', who will frequently travel over city and county boundaries to make sure of finding a class where they will be unrecognized, are likely to be more in need of reassurance and support than a group of adults of all ages and intelligence who come into a local institute for the relaxation and creative enjoyment of the woodwork class once a week.

But whatever the situation, there is likely to be some tension if there is real learning. Learning takes place best in a calm, unworried and friendly atmosphere. This is the tone to establish right from the start and to maintain all the way through the course. Strategies for the first class, a uniquely important occasion in teaching adults, are discussed fully in Chapter 7, but the same basic principles of consciously relaxed friendliness should always be applied.

The tutor's role

Friendliness is important, but it only goes part of the way towards reducing adult anxieties. It is even more important to make sure that students are immediately rewarded when they get something right, to see that everybody is drawn into the discussion, and to devise tasks that everyone can get right. In a discussion, for instance, 'getting something right' can be simply drawing appreciative comments from other students and the tutor – 'Yes, that's an interesting idea', or 'As Mrs Smith said last week', or 'You remember Mr Jones's argument was' – such small and apparently trifling tokens of interest and respect can be important ways of lowering tension and anxiety in adults. At first they must come from you, but it is noticeable that in the most productive and enjoyable adult classes, the role of giving this sort of 'reward' is frequently assumed by other students.

Sometimes you will find it necessary to resort to more direct ways of reducing individual anxiety. You may find it useful to make constant offers of individual assistance to those who might admit to needing it. Obviously there are limits in time and energy to how much of this intensive help you can actually give. Not all of it can be done in class, otherwise other students suffer. Help that can properly be offered outside the main class-time might be to mark extra work, to have all look at a previously written essay, to stay behind after a class to explain a basic principle which a few students do not understand, to prepare individual worksheets for some students to do in their own time, or to lend books and articles. Perhaps the form the help takes does not matter as much as your obvious willingness to offer it and to undertake it when requested.

Sometimes teachers can be so conscious of the need to alleviate anxiety that they go to the other extreme – their classes are so friendly that no learning is done at all, because the teacher never dares to challenge the students. Such teachers have played themselves out of a role. Although on the surface these classes seem to be pleasant enough, they often disintegrate in sheer frustration when the students begin to realize that in spite of the pleasant, even self-congratulatory atmosphere, nothing has been accomplished.

At the other end of the spectrum I have heard some teachers, or more particularly some trainers, press the claims of deliberately whipping up anxiety in adult students. 'Keeps them on their toes to be a bit worried, and therefore does them good' is how the argument usually goes. Often this is another way of saying, 'This is how I was taught, and this is how I'm going to teach', implying further that it is only by the effort of the teacher who constantly goads the class into action that work is done at all. Nobody is claiming that adults should be so relaxed that they go to sleep or don't care, but deliberately to encourage worry is counter-productive. Tutors who try it in classes where the students come voluntarily will soon find themselves without a class.

Ageing

Anxiety can be overcome, but you may find yourself dealing with more subtly destructive forces in the learner's own mind, and this is the adult student's belief that his intellectual powers inevitably suffer serious decay with age. Teachers of languages, for instance, or teachers of any subject where students believe memorizing to be involved, will frequently find themselves being told, and not only by the elderly, 'I can't remember things very easily now – it just won't go in', or 'I'm afraid I'm just not as bright as I used to be'. Even students who say nothing on the topic may secretly be wondering whether their struggles with a subject may not be caused by some inevitable declines of their abilities with age.

The phenomenon has been noticed by those researchers who have investigated the effects of ageing on learning. One of the most celebrated of these research projects was conducted by A. T. Welford at Oxford between 1946 and 1956. In describing his results and methods, Welford comments wryly on the difficulties this belief creates for the researcher:

> Most investigators have found difficulty in obtaining middle-aged and old subjects. It is fairly easy to obtain men in their twenties, but in the thirties and over they become increasingly unwilling. Many plead lack of time, or raise other difficulties, or agree to come, then forget. These pleas are, of course, sometimes well justified, but it is quite clear that in most cases they are excuses and that the real reason for unwillingness is fear of being tested and in particular of doing badly and appearing foolish. They seem to know well the popular opinion that as one advances through middle age one's ability falls, and do not wish to have this demonstrated upon themselves.
>
> The fear manifests itself in several ways. For example, typical remarks made by older subjects before being tested are: 'You don't really want me, do you? I shan't be very good.' 'You can't expect too much of me; after all I'm nearly sixty.' 'So this is where you make a fool of me, is it?' After being tested, older subjects almost always ask how they have done and demand to know how their results compare with the average. . . . Visible relief and pleasure are frequently shown by older subjects upon being told they have 'done well'. Yet even when told this may criticize their performances and produce reasons, such as eyestrain, tiredness or preoccupation with other problems, for not having done better. Frequently their actual performances in no way merit this self-criticism.*

Welford was describing an experimental situation where his subjects were being asking to participate in something unfamiliar, where the 'testing' element was likely to be paramount in the

* A. T. Welford. *Ageing and Human Skill*, Oxford University Press, 1958.

subjects' minds because they knew what the researchers were investigating. In such a situation the subjects were likely to be extremely touchy about the relationship between their age and their performance. But this is not so far removed from the classroom situation; indeed the reactions of Welford's subjects may only be unusual in their frankness. Under pressure his subjects may have shown beliefs that many older adult students have, but never quite voice in the classroom.

Whatever your students may think, there is plenty of powerful popular reinforcement for the idea that, as Shakespeare's Dogberry asserted, 'when the age is in, the wit is out'. Many firms make public their policy of not recruiting anyone over thirty-five, and in spite of the fact that, for instance, airlines will retrain pilots in their fifties to fly new aircraft, it is undoubtedly true that there is a prejudice against the middle-aged and elderly at work. Proverbs like 'You can't teach an old dog new tricks' are damaging enough in their way, but perhaps even more harm comes from the words of those academics who have given a certain gloss to the same thought. One of the most famous of these pronouncements came from Sir William Osler in 1905. Osler was a celebrated physician and Professor of Medicine, and when he retired from the Johns Hopkins University at the age of fifty-five to take up a new appointment at Oxford he made a semi-serious speech, jokingly advocating chloroforming those over sixty, and more seriously advising letting the younger men get on with the real business of the world.

> The effective, moving, vitalizing work of the world is done between the ages of twenty-five and forty – these fifteen golden years of plenty, the anabolic or constructive period, in which there is always a balance in the mental bank and the credit is still good.

Osler was apparently deeply hurt at the torrent of abusive letters and caustic comments that followed newspaper headlines such as 'Osler Recommends Chloroform at Sixty', but 'Oslerism' had by then entered popular mythology, and for years afterwards people who had never read his speech quoted what they imagined he had said.

In the 1960s, the anthropologist Edmund Leach achieved in his own words a surprising *succès de scandale* not dissimilar to that created more innocently by Osler over sixty years before. In the Reith Lectures for 1967, Leach spoke coolly but provocatively of the way galloping technological change was creating entirely new kinds of knowledge, and how it was making the opinions and skills of the elderly irrelevant to present-day and future life:

> In our runaway world, no one much over the age of forty-five is really fit to teach anyone anything. And that includes me. I am fifty-seven. It is hard to accept but that's just the point . . .
>
> Medical science is steadily increasing the expectation of life and this, combined with the concentration of industry into larger and larger units, is having the effect that an ever greater proportion of the final power of decision is being concentrated into the hands of very old men, which is the worst possible way of facing the problems of a rapidly changing future. Since those who hold offices of power will never willingly give them up, I believe that there is only one solution to this problem. The young must somehow or other enforce quite arbitrary rules of early retirement. In those parts of our systems which are concerned with research and technological development, either in education, or in industry, or in politics, no one should be allowed to hold any kind of responsible administrative office once he has passed the age of fifty-five.*

The total effect of the adult student's own and other people's belief in his declining ability to learn with age may create quite severe difficulties, especially if you are teaching a class where older people predominate. Students may use their age as a crutch to avoid the discomfort of real learning; their whole attitude may imply 'You mustn't work me hard, because I'm old'. They may unconsciously be working at very much less than full pressure because they are afraid that if they really try they may really fail; they have lost confidence in their ability to work at full intellectual capacity.

If you are faced with this situation you must somehow encourage learners to believe that although there is some decrease in intellectual capacity with age, this is negligible compared with more important factors such as their motivation now. Teachers will say this bluntly to students, but they run the risk of having a student say, 'But I never got much education and I was never very bright in the first place, so what hope is there for me now?' Brightly encouraging remarks from a tutor may have their place, but there is nothing

* Edmund Leach, *A Runaway World?*, BBC Publications, 1968.

to equal the encouragement students feel when they can see for themselves that they are making progress. Designing a situation where this can happen will be one of your strongest weapons against anxiety in older students.

Even so, it is bound to be true for many adults that we feel some loss of confidence as our physical appearance changes with age; we may feel depressed about the loss of responsibility as our children grow up, or anxious about whether computerization is likely to do us out of a job. We may be bitter or disillusioned as ambitions remain unfulfilled, a situation not improved by our current obsession with youth and youthful achievement. This is a gloomy picture, an exaggerated one perhaps, but research studies tend to support the idea of 'crisis' with aging. Indeed some people suggest that we ought to be much less concerned with the stresses and problems of the adolescent and much more concerned with those of the middle-aged and elderly.

Social background

Adult learners' attitudes towards themselves are also deeply affected by social class. One of the most revealing themes in Margaret Powell's frank and funny autobiographical books* – unique and unpretentious pieces of sociological material – is how absolute and unchangeable the social structure seemed to a domestic servant. The privileges of education, like privileges of comfort, were accepted as being the natural prerogative of the rich. It took Margaret Powell, a sturdy and tireless spirit, most of a lifetime to reach the stage where she could aspire even to O-level English, and her account in *Climbing the Stairs* of her brushes with adult education ought to be read by every teacher. Many who were less confident, less persistent, have never even come that far.

Working-class attitudes

Statistics have shown again and again how thousands of able working-class children drop out of full-time education. For instance, the percentage of working-class children now going to university is much the same as it was before 1939. The reasons are obviously

* *Below Stairs*, Peter Davies, 1968; *Climbing the Stairs*, Peter Davies, 1969.

complicated, but if a home has few books, if parents see the school as remote and even hostile, if simple information about education is lacking (for example, that grants are available for university students) then it is likely that children in such a home will drop out of education early and go into jobs much less demanding than their abilities would warrant. Not all working-class children have the constant prodding and support from their parents that many middle-class children have, and financial considerations may press hard. The practice of streaming by ability in schools quickly becomes a self-fulfilling prophecy, and children's records show that once children are graded 'C stream' they live down to what teachers expect of C-stream children. They grow into adults incapable of making A-stream responses.

It is difficult to generalize here and exceptions are legion, but several studies show not only the detailed mechanisms of such processes but also how personality patterns established in childhood and contributed to by education and social class together tend to encourage an attitude where many working-class people think that education is not for them. They tend to believe that they are meant to be followers rather than leaders, expecting to be dominated and controlled, often resentfully, but still playing the subordinate role. The C-stream child may grow up to be an adult who can only find a menial job, and many people have pointed out how working-class people whose education and jobs have accustomed them to being ordered and controlled by other people may find it difficult as adults in education to assume responsibility themselves. On the other hand, middle-class people will tend not to be afraid of headmasters, to know their way around education, and indeed will even describe the advantages of something like public-school education in terms of its having been an 'education for leadership'.

This is a caricatured view of a complex social class structure, but social class is one important part of adult learners' backgrounds and it will affect the way they approach learning. In many cases it will determine whether they undertake further education at all, since social class is a major factor in distinguishing those who are participants in adult education and those who are not. Given that adult education appeals strongly to the middle class and to those who already have a good education, it should not surprise anyone that class will affect students in the learning situation itself, influencing the amount of responsibility students feel they can undertake for their own learning and the way they react to the tutor and to other students.

Memories of school

Whatever their social class, all adult students come to education with well-developed sets of expectations about what it will be like. Inevitably, these expectations are governed very largely by their experience of education as a child, and these experiences will considerably influence the way tutors are able to conduct the class.

In industry there may, for instance, be severe problems with adults who are working in semi-skilled jobs and have to be retrained to keep a job at all. Many of these people may be the grown-up products of the type of education whose desperate shortcomings John Partridge described so well in his closely observed account of one year in the life of a secondary modern school.* His comments on the low level of motivation towards learning in the school can stand as a reminder to the adult tutor or training officer of attitudes that may be even more deeply entrenched in maturity:

> Firstly, English education, as seen by these boys, consists of preparing for examinations and little else; but these are the boys who have failed every test and examination they have ever taken, so that asking these boys to take their work seriously is like suggesting to prisoners of war that they should voluntarily undertake eight hours daily combat training. Since we spend so much time and energy on grading and examining children, we can hardly expect those who have constantly failed to be exceptionally keen for the next round.

This type of child is all too happy to be waved off the school premises at the minimum legal age. As an adult he may have a deep suspicion of 'education', and is certainly unlikely to enrol voluntarily for 'night school', even if it might be of direct vocational advantage if he did.

In industry, where for various reasons he may be obliged to undertake further education, tremendous allowances must be made for his likely attitudes. For instance, no one will use the word

*John Partridge, *Life in a Secondary Modern School*, Gollancz, 1966; Penguin, 1968.

'education' because that sounds too much like studying a subject for its own sake. Instead it will be called 'training', which is not so alarming, and many 'trainers' will be anxious to stress their affinities with the chap on the shop floor. They will go to great pains to avoid resembling either the tweedy, seedy, patched-elbowed teacher-figure of tradition, or the 'overdressed arrogant men who use long words to embarrass and trap people' which one child described in a competition on 'The school that I'd like'.*

Instead, many trainers go to almost comic lengths to create a kind of Andy Capp atmosphere where social distance is instantly reduced and where the idea is that if attitudes to the tutor can be changed, that is at least one barrier out of the way. Oddly enough, this type of adult student may not be at all resistant to 'new' methods and trainers play one of their strongest cards when they are able to say that the methods *are* new, that they do work, that they will be totally unlike anything the adult experienced at school. This kind of announcement can bring nothing but relief to adults who loathed and detested almost every moment at school, and whose dread of industrial training can largely be reduced to a fear of it turning out to be just like school.

Student expectations

Those who were a little luckier in their parents' social status, or more fortunate in their previous educational experiences, may bring with them equally firm ideas of what they expect from a teacher and his methods. Firstly, in spite of wanting due deference paid to the fact that they are adults, many adult students may still feel a teacher ought to be a rather remote, god-like figure. They may consider it rather improper for a teacher to be too friendly. Confusion and embarrassment sometimes result from your first attempts to establish a relaxed atmosphere – for these students it is too much like seeing 'Sir' pick his nose or engage in any other ordinary human activity. Fortunately this sort of shyness is easily broken down, especially in a group which contains plenty of students who have attended other courses and who can show newcomers how to put tutors in their places.

Secondly, and in practice inextricably mixed with attitudes to

* Edward Blishen (ed.), *The School that I'd Like*, Penguin, 1969.

your role, students may have firm expectations about teaching methods based again on their experience at school or in higher education. Even those who had only modest success academically are still likely to feel that the methods they already know are best because they are the only ones already familiar.

A student who has been out of touch with education for a long time, or who is under a misapprehension about 'modern' methods, may fiercely resist your attempts to introduce a different kind of education, even though, paradoxically, the 'new' methods may be clearly both more enjoyable and in the long run more effective. This particularly applies to subjects with which adults have already had some acquaintance. Although many adult students will come to classes in, say, English because previous methods have failed, they will expect the conventional methods with grammar to be employed, because they blame themselves for previous failure, not the teaching method. They frequently think that if only the same method could be employed but more intensively, then all their problems would be solved. They may also feel, as a result no doubt of the irrelevance of much of their previous education, that learning and their own lives have nothing in common, that 'real' education is something remote and separate. Your attempts to solicit and 'use' your students' own experience of life may for this reason meet with incomprehension. One English teacher describes here the practical difficulties these sorts of problems created on a course in English:

> Most of the class, but especially the overseas students, felt that I ought to be teaching them in the formal notes-on-the-blackboard, do-this-and-you-will-be-successful style they remembered from their own schooldays. They found it difficult to grasp the fact that copying into notebooks pious dicta on what constitutes an essay is no substitute for trying to write one. Only slowly have they come to realize that they have each amassed a store of experiences which, though apparently trivial, could supply them with essay material for the year. For the first month I read their essays with despair; the prospect of finding a mark scheme to cover such a wide range seemed impossible. Yet this, too, they seemed to regard as essential, and I soon discovered that all my tactfully worded suggestions for improving style and content, punctuation and spelling, were regarded as mere stalling on my part, a refusal to get down to the

real business of the course. Eventually the hard core of enthusiasts who survived after Christmas accepted my methods. I, too, had learned to compromise and in some measure give the sort of instruction they expected in return for a show of participation from them.

Other versions of the same basic situation may be found throughout the whole range of adult education: students who come to learn languages and are disconcerted *not* to be given lists of irregular verbs to memorize; trainees in industry who expect to be *told* how to understand a chemical process and are surprised to find themselves faced with open learning instead; people who come to art classes thinking that the first thing the teacher will do is to expound on the laws of perspective and are astonished to find instead that they are painting pictures straight away; literature students who may think that there is a 'correct' view of a novel or play and that somehow the tutor will convey this to them without any real thought being necessary or proper on their part.

Wherever adult education happens there may be a discrepancy between what the students expect and what you propose to do. The older the students are, the more their previous experience was likely to have been 'passive', since they were at school when the emphasis was on teaching rather than learning, and education was regarded as something that was done to you, and not something to which you made a major contribution yourself.

Frequently, a change of method will be welcomed with delight by adult students, but sometimes the adult's longing for the 'old' methods has deep roots, not just in previous education but in the motive for joining. Such students may sit patiently enough through several weeks of 'modern' method, still waiting for you to reveal the magic key which will effortlessly unlock every secret of the subject. Because of this, they may have paid no attention to what has been happening in the class – it has been brushed aside as padding.

Similarly, attempts by craft teachers to broaden the subject by introducing discussion on materials or standards may meet with polite tolerance, while students wait for a teacher to get back to what they think is the more important task of teaching them how to cut out a dress or decoke an engine. In craft classes students may expect individual attention and may be puzzled or hurt at the teacher's attempts to introduce methods where group teaching and learning is established. Even in sophisticated classes the students may expect the teacher to dominate and control a discussion to a greater extent than he may feel right. The students may interpret this behaviour as intellectual feebleness or laziness.

This is why it is essential to discuss right at the beginning not only the course and syllabus but also the method of teaching, so that students know what to expect (this point is developed in Chapter 7). It would be very rare indeed to find an adult class stubbornly unwilling even to try an unfamiliar method, but the method itself, like the course, should be constantly under review by you and your students and the appropriate modifications made by both parties:

> I was teaching French to children in a grammar school during the day, using what I considered to be a very good audio-visual method. I saw no reason why my adult class should not learn the same way and they very nobly agreed to try.
>
> I met my first snag in the first five minutes – no books. No books? They demand books, nicely, of course. I say they cannot have books until at least the sixth week when they will be familiar with certain sounds and patterns. Rebellion subsides. Second snag – five minutes later – several of them sneakily trying to write things down according to some dreadful phonetic script of their own. I explain about listening and speaking, they explain they must see things written down, otherwise they can't remember. We have this very polite battle lasting three weeks. They begin to see the advantages of the language lab and slide projector and the constant repetition – variation – drilling, I begin to see that they really do need the reassurance of the book. On the fourth week I give out books, they sigh with relief as at the appearance of old friends, pronunciation slips a bit, but general progress seems to be faster. It's not Direct Method, but it seems to suit my class.

Checklist

Have you made plans to defuse the anxieties of your students? ☐

Will your teaching methods allow learners' previous experience to be acknowledged? ☐

used? ☐

Is the atmosphere of your sessions consciously 'friendly'? ☐

Will learners immediately be 'rewarded' for their contributions? ☐

Do you make it clear that you are available for additional help if individuals encounter difficulties? ☐

Does the work allow students to see for themselves that they are making progress? ☐

Do you know the learners well enough to be familiar with their expectations of the class? ☐

Have you made plans to overcome any problems this could cause? ☐

2

What makes adults want to learn?

It's so obvious really, but it must be stated: unless you are motivated, you will not and cannot learn. As a tutor you therefore must tap into and keep refreshing the motivation of your students, otherwise the class will collapse.

I have recently had an exasperating experience with one of my cats. Bluebell is a British Short-hair of stunning good looks but is living proof that a long pedigree and physical beauty do not guarantee intelligence. She has always been a slow learner, and a cat of exasperating blankness. She decided recently that her dirt tray was no longer a suitable place to deposit her faeces and began using a particular place on the carpet instead. Shouting, smacking and speaking sternly have no effect on cats, they simply become more adept and sly at defeating you. Instead, I patiently waited after meals for her to approach the favoured spot of carpet, picked her up gently but firmly, and carried her to her tray. This did not work. She would use the tray under protest, but after the next meal would wander blandly towards 'her' carpet again. Why was my 'training' a failure? Because Bluebell had no motivation whatever to please me. Cats, unlike dogs, are not pack animals and have no reason to worry about currying our favour. So I had to think again. What was her motive for using the carpet? Suddenly it dawned on me that the offence occurred most often when the tray had already been visited by her daughter: fastidiousness was the problem. Scrupulous removal of this evidence combined with steady supervision produced instant improvement.

You may feel that this example has no bearing on human motivation, but I believe it does. Bluebell had her own reasons for her irritating lapses. I could not oblige her to accept my rules until I had uncovered what her motivation was. Human beings are hundreds of times more devious and subtle, but the basics of learning are the same for humans and animals: to learn you must be motivated. To teach, you must uncover, create and sustain the motivation.

Some tutors feel that just being exposed to the subject is enough: people will 'learn by stealth'. While no doubt we could all quote some examples of this happening, it is not an efficient or sensible way to proceed. When involved in training tutors of adults in London, I have sometimes tried this experiment: write down from memory the colours and alphabetical breakdown of the London telephone directories. Even though most Londoners use the directories constantly, the number of people who achieved a totally correct answer was usually only around 10 per cent. Why? Because most of us have absolutely no motivation for 'learning' the link between the alphabetical breakdown and the colour or even what the colours are. It is not a useful piece of knowledge, so even though we are constantly exposed to the information we do not 'learn' it.

Lack of, or wilting, motivation is one of the main reasons why learning fails:

> At first my YTS students *loathed* being in college. They hated school, they regarded YTS as a poor substitute for a job and were resentful about being put back in a situation which they thought would be just like school again. The first week was a real struggle: trying to get them to see that it would all be quite different if only they'd give it a chance.
>
> Basically they didn't know *why* they were doing the course. It had been decreed from 'on high' that all managers above a certain level had to do 'computer appreciation', but no attempt had been made to sell them any of the practical benefits they would gain. The opening sessions were always grim: stony faces and looking at watches and 'when's coffee?'!
>
> I had started out with high hopes that what I might achieve was the kind of experience that would help me run meetings better. Instead all I had was an academic analysis of 'Roles People Play'. It was very boring and I felt like leaving at lunchtime. Guilt about how much it was costing my company for the two days was the only thing that kept me there.

These are examples of the devastating effect of ignoring the importance of motivation. However, the other side of this coin is how wonderfully sustaining strong motivation can be, especially when it is fanned by an expert tutor:

> My aim is to pass GCSE English because that is what my son is doing. I have been able to help him a lot, and I suddenly realized I might be able to do it myself. I went to a secondary modern school as a child and they didn't do O levels. I have always had it in my head that there was something special about O-level English, and I was absolutely determined to achieve it. It has been very hard because of all the course work, and also because I haven't done any formal learning for such a long time. What has sustained me is the thought of actually getting that certificate. My tutor has been wonderful. She has praised us, nagged us and has kept dangling the thought of THE PASS at the end!

> People often ask me what keeps me going, as everyone now seems to appreciate how hard it is to do Open University work on top of everything else that's going on in your life. It is very hard work, but it's simple really: I always regretted that I had to leave school at 17. My stepmother and I did not get on and she made it clear that I was a financial burden, so university was out of the question. She also implied that I was not bright enough. Although she's been dead for many years now, I know that one of my principal motivators is to prove her wrong on the second count, and to feel, on the first, that this is something I deserve and owe to myself. I *will* do it!

Students come to education for many reasons, and not always the simple and obvious ones. There is no such thing as a 'disreputable' motive for joining a class or course. All reasons are acceptable because any motivation is better than none.

It is important to accept this fundamental truth. Almost all adult learners come freely to classes: this is one of the main features that distinguishes them from children who, by statute, have to receive education from five to sixteen. Very, very few adults come to classes or courses because they have been enrolled reluctantly. I have never yet met or taught a group where the great majority were not there of their own free will: most usually they are 100 per cent volunteers. The implication of this is that they are also free to leave. (The one exception may be people on government training schemes, who sometimes complain that they are 'trapped' into attending courses.)

All of them will be able to think of attractive alternative ways they might be spending their time, and it will not always be easy to squeeze in the commitment to the class:

> I have a towering in-tray. I'm trying not to think about it while I'm here.
>
> What do I give up to get here? Watching *EastEnders*! Also cash. The petrol is expensive.
>
> At the end of a long day there are great attractions to just sliding off to the pub with the others. It takes discipline to come here instead!
>
> Some kids just slouch around or stay in bed all day. I do find it difficult to get up sometimes, but I'm hoping this course will help me find a job.

Glancing over the great range of motives that adults bring with them to learning, their only unifying feature often seems to be their enormous variety. The simplest motives are the 'extrinsic' ones: the learning that seems demanded by the learner's situation. Here are some of the most common:

- *Promotion* may depend on passing an exam or doing a course. This is the case, for instance, in the police force, whose exam system is designed to make sure that promoted personnel have the knowledge required to do the new job; it does not guarantee them the post.
- *Entry to a new career* may depend on basic qualifications. For instance, jobs in accountancy will demand ACCA certificates, junior jobs in Personnel may depend on the successful candidate's willingness to study part-time for the IPM's Certificate in Personnel Management.
- *More money* may automatically be offered to people who have attended a course or achieved a qualification. The early dominance of non-graduate teachers among Open University students was at least partly explained by the fact the graduates were paid more.
- *Change* is a powerful motivator which may lead an employer to offer or to insist on training. One of the reasons we resist change is that we are afraid we will not know what to do in the new system. A library is computerizing book issue. The librarians want to

> cling to their date stamps and card tickets because, they say, they loathe the noise made by the bar-coding pencil. This may be so, but the underlying reasons probably have more to do with their fear of computers. A good training course will show them that they do not need to understand megabytes in order to operate the new system effectively. The change from O-level to GCSE involved thousands of teachers in training because the new exam was radically different from the old. The training was most successful when it helped teachers confront their reluctance to leave the old system by showing them clearly how to operate the new one.

Motivation like this is clear-cut and easy to understand. The muddier area of so-called 'intrinsic' motivation is both more tricky and more rewarding. Adult education specializing in 'leisure' subjects has always had a reputation, possibly undeserved, for attracting the bored and the lonely. Edna Smith, Warden of a short-term residential college for adults once quoted this sad evidence that such people really do exist:

> Would you please book me for courses 26, 27, 28, 29, 30, 32, 34, 35, 37, 38, 41, all on your current list. If you send me the application forms I will fill them in, but I am sending the cheque now to make sure of getting in.*

Equally, there are legends about whole groups of friends and neighbours who shop around at enrolment time for a class, any class, that will take them all. Some students will certainly have social motives for joining, and will, if asked, stated their loneliness unequivocally.

> I joined an evening class about six years ago for the simple reason that I felt lonely at the time and needed social contact. The subject was incidental – in this case the history of London. The lecturer was dull, spending the whole time either reading from a book or just talking at us. Nevertheless I must have obtained something from the class because I've been interested in the subject ever since.

If you encounter such motives, I feel the healthy reaction is, 'so what?' Remember the student does not have to be in your class. He

* Edna Smith, 'New courses for "old hands"', *Adult Education*, vol. 40, no. 5, 1968.

or she has positively chosen your class rather than any other, and in preference to spending the time at a disco, at bingo or down at the pub, all excellent ways of meeting other people. Such students are nearly always a good yeast in the group: they work hard at getting to know other people, join in everything enthusiastically and can be excellent 'moles' about what is going on under the surface of an apparently tranquil group.

Many students come to learning with a motivation which includes the wish to test themselves against a yardstick of academic difficulty. 'Am I the kind of person who could get GCSE Maths?' 'I should like to be able to say that I can speak Mandarin.' 'I know that it will be a hard slog to achieve this BTec Certificate, but having wasted so much time at school, I feel I have to prove to myself that I am up to it.' For students like these, the subject is less interesting than what they are proving to themselves by achieving something they and the outside world think difficult.

Some motives are straightforwardly to do with remedying some deficiency – real or imagined – which must now be faced.

> I read OK, but writing was just a torment. My wife filled up every form for me, and anything at work that had to be written down, I'd get one of my mates to do on the quiet. When my son was six he began learning 'writing' at school, and he just couldn't understand why I wouldn't 'play writing' with him. He pestered me so much that I couldn't bear the shame of it any more. We got in touch with the local scheme and they found me a tutor. It was much, much easier than I'd imagined. The worst bit was admitting to someone outside the family that I couldn't write.

This story, and thousands of others like it, was behind the modest success of the Adult Literacy Campaign. Even admitting to such painful failure defeats most adults, which is why the Campaign found it much easier to recruit volunteer tutors than it did to find students. In spite of all the publicity and a well-coordinated campaign, only 50,000 students came forward for teaching, when estimates of the need varied from 1 to 6 million. One of the reasons for the failure of the MSC's Job Training Scheme is often given as the extraordinarily high rate (25 per cent) of functional illiteracy (that is, not necessarily complete reading failure but enough difficulty to prove handicapping) found by the scheme among its target clientele.

Putting it right proved too greedy on the meagre resources given to managing agents, and tackling the problem of non-readers and writers in a literate society remains a high priority for all government training schemes present and future.

Straightforward remedial motives will remain among the most uncommon that most tutors will uncover in their classrooms, in spite of schemes like YTS and the Employment Training programme. This is because even very young adults are expert at concealing failure. As we get older we become ever more skilled at hiding what we don't know, and avoiding the occasions which would reveal it. Survey after survey shows that the better educated you are, the more likely you are to look for more education, and the less well educated you are, the more likely you are to avoid it. Even the Open University, with its determined efforts to live up to the openness of its title, has failed to break this cycle. The majority of OU students have from the beginning fallen into the 'better educated than average' category and still do.

Most adult learning groups will contain some people who are addicted to learning 'for its own sake'. These perpetual joiners are usually a pleasure to teach, though their underlying motives can remain mysterious:

> Why did Mr P enrol for psychology one year, philosophy the next, then – and this was a tantalizing mystery – economical cookery? His only explanation was that he 'just loved learning'. I knew that his family had been well-off but had had eccentric views about education and had 'not believed in' universities. Perhaps he was making up for this, but he was a cheerful and loyal student well into his seventies!

> About half way through my OU degree, I realised that I had proved I could do it, and I didn't really 'need' to go on. By then I was thoroughly hooked – I couldn't give it up. I just loved the feeling that I was plugging in to the best academic knowledge in such a wide range of subjects. As soon as I got the degree, I enrolled for something else.

> I have always loved learning. It gives me the kick other people might obtain from cocaine or booze. The loss of my library tickets would be a major tragedy; I have bought many part works from volume 1 to volume 50 and I own an *Encyclopaedia*

> *Britannica*, as well as joining courses and classes whenever they seem to be on some intriguing subject. Medieval London, Lakeland Poets, Economic Problems of Underdeveloped Countries . . . I've done them all!

One group makes a neat bridge between 'have to' learners and 'want to' learners. These are the ever-growing numbers of women 'returners'. Social change has made this group eager for education and training. The upwardly spiralling divorce rate and the increase in single-parenthood means that economic independence is a necessity, not a luxury, and a good job often needs to be preceded by good education and training.

> My last job was as a secretary. That was 18 years ago. Now my marriage is breaking up and my son is in his first year at university. My husband does not earn a lot of money, and in any case I am determined not to accept a penny from him, except maintenance for our daughter. I see the Access course I'm on as my main hope of getting back into proper employment. I've had jobs but they've been tin-pot, part-time ones, 'unreal' and badly paid. I've simply *got* to get some proper training.

> I never really wanted to give up work, but I had no choice – we just couldn't afford childminders and in any case I honestly felt I was the best possible person to bring up our children. But being at home has been stultifying mentally, much as I've loved seeing my children grow and develop. Now I'm absolutely longing to get back to work – but to what work? I don't want to go back into banking. I've always loved sewing and been good at it. So I'm doing a soft furnishing and upholstery course at a very good London College, and I'm planning to start a small business with a friend – the prospects look good. London is full of people who want curtains, blinds and loose covers, but I'm frightened of making mistakes. That's why it's worth learning to do it properly.

These learners are a rich pool of talent for trainers and adult educators. They may be divorced and separated women desperate to be self-supporting, or women still married but eager to return to the 'real' world of work. Many such women find that their careers have been sabotaged by child-rearing. Their skills are out of date, their confidence is sapped by feeling that, because they are not paid for what they do, they themselves must be valueless.

What these women want is qualifications and self-confidence; what they need is often a bit different: the assertiveness that will help them speak for themselves after so many years of being described solely as someone's wife or someone's mother.

Whatever the motivation, find out what it is by asking direct, by getting students to fill in a form or by discussing it as part of the course. It will help you plan the work so that it has immediate benefits for the students. If the group has a high number of 'social' attenders, then make sure that discussion and activity have a solid place in the programme together with opportunities for socializing. Where there are large numbers of 'lovers of learning', give them meaty assignments which take them down academic routes. If examinations are part of the programme then it is not a 'betrayal' of the subject to devote substantial time to learning examination technique.

Finding out what motivation your students have is essential for another reason – you may discover that some of them are in absolutely the wrong class. A learner set on GCSE Maths is not going to get there with a 'Modern Maths for Parents' group. Early candid counselling and directing to other courses where necessary will save a lot of mutual heartache later. Be prepared, though, to accept that some students recognize that their proposed route is indirect: they may still be capable of thriving in a group which seems a long way from their ultimate goal.

When thinking about student motivation in learning, there are some helpful notions from the theory and practice of management. Why do people work at all? What makes work satisfying?

First, it is worth considering Herzberg's 'hygiene' and 'satisfier' theories.* Imagine you are working in a dank, cold noisy environment with substandard equipment. You are not likely to feel satisfied with your job. Now imagine that a wand is waved and the work environment becomes clean, warm, well ventilated and the equipment excellent. Is this likely to make you happy in your work? Not necessarily. These elements are the 'hygiene' factors, prone to making you unhappy if they are neglected, but not in themselves

* F. Hertzberg *et al.*, *The Motivation to Work*, 2nd Edition, John Wiley, 1959.

capable of making work satisfying. The features of work that give people real reward are those that offer them genuine responsibility and the opportunity for growth and self-development.

These theories, like all the best social psychology, seem obvious once stated. They seemed revolutionary when first voiced, as there were plenty of managers then (and sadly there still are) who, like some of their counterparts in teaching, had a low view of human nature and believed that we are all basically workshy: what motivates us, according to this school is a wish to avoid pain – to achieve the best result for the least possible effort. Therefore, we should be bullied into shape with sanctions and threats. Such theories make responsibility for yourself – the basic aim of all adult learning – virtually impossible to achieve. I do not recommend it as a helpful way to think about teaching.

Another useful theory about work and learning is 'expectancy theory'. This suggests that motivation is closely linked with the idea of 'fair reward' that people expect from their effort. What 'fair reward' are people getting from your classes? Not getting enough may well explain why people leave.

Management practice can also lend teachers some useful ideas for analysing what is happening when things go wrong. Just as a manager should be alert to the symptoms of demotivation in a workforce, so a sensitive tutor will react to the same signs in a class. The danger signals are similar: lateness, absenteeism, deterioration in the quality of work, challenges to discipline:

> The class started off with 20 very keen members. It was a tough course, but the tutor did not help. His analysis seemed remote from the essays we were supposed to do, he talked to the blackboard instead of to us; usually only about four other people spoke. Every meeting there was a muddle about the room we were in, so we always started late. By the third meeting people were coming in up to an hour late and the group was down to ten. Several people submitted work which they said they knew was poor, but said they didn't care: one or two people indulged in childish muttering while the tutor was talking – it was a disaster, the whole thing.

What can be done to arrest a situation like this? If your students stop coming to your class or are persistently late, you must assume, until proved otherwise, that they do not like the class enough to make the effort to turn up on time or even at all.

Students will offer excuses and some will be perfectly genuine: moving house, serious illness, or urgent domestic crises. More often, the excuse is just that, a reluctance to say candidly that the class was boring or disappointing and that the initial motivation has trickled away.

It is always worth contacting absentees. There is some research to suggest that many learners can be missing for six weeks or more, but still regard themselves as members of the group, intending to return at some point. A friendly postcard may be the prompt they need. A phone call is even better: that way you can actually ask what they felt about the class.

Reading this chapter, I am struck by the artificiality of the categories I have created, however much they may help you recognize initial motivation in your students. My own experience tells me that such divisions are only superficially helpful, for a number of reasons.

First, initial motivation is just that: the bundle of hopes that students bring to the first few classes. It can be changed. In any case, in a successful class it should develop and grow and may become unrecognizable by the end of the course. In an unsuccessful class it may shrivel and die: this is a defeat for the tutor.

Second, all motives are mixed. The learner who claims only to want to pass an A level to even the score with a more successful sibling may also need to acquire the A level for professional reasons. The intelligent non-reader trapped into admitting the need for tuition may equally be ready to expand into far more intellectual territory for its own sake.

Finally, these categories only tell us what students *think* their motivation is. But perhaps the truth is simpler. Learning is a natural part of living and growing. It can continue to hold us in thrall throughout our lives because every change, every stage, offers us challenges, which means opportunities for extending and growing. To learn and master a skill, a piece of knowledge, to acquire a new outlook on a problem is a normal and fundamentally satisfying human process. For myself, I am as proud of now being able to swim 1,000 metres elegantly and swiftly as I am to have passed an Open University examination. Both cost me a great deal of time and effort. My true motivation is opaque to me, but does it really matter? I was ready for learning, I often found the process frustrating; I was humbled by my inability to leave the 'learning plateaux' behind at key stages, but I persisted. Now I take pleasure in knowing that the result was worth while. Surely this is what it is all about. Learning is part of a circuit that is one of life's fundamental pleasures: the tutor's role is to keep the current flowing.

Checklist on motivation

Do you know the reasons all your students have given for joining the class? ☐

Have they all been asked to state their personal goals – i.e. what they hope to have achieved by the end of the course? ☐

Do you have a system for feedback on motivation during the course? ☐

Is there provision at the end of the course for feedback on whether they feel they achieved their goals? ☐

Do you have a system for counselling/advising students whose motivation/goals are not well-matched to yours for the group? ☐

Do you have a system for monitoring and controlling

- latecomers? ☐
- poor work? ☐
- inattentiveness? ☐

Do you monitor and contact absentees? ☐

3

How do adults learn?

It has in fact been established that if we were to reverse the natural order of things and keep children away from school while sending their parents there instead, we could teach the parents the same thing for about a quarter of the expenditure in time and money.

John McLeish

I hear and I forget
I see and I remember
I do and I understand
Old Chinese Proverb

Let's assume that your students are highly motivated. You understand that they might be feeling anxious and you have techniques ready to allay their fears. But this still leaves other questions unanswered. How do you guide your learners through the substance of your subject? What are the best ways to engage their interest? Is it actually harder for adults than children to learn quickly? Are there any special methods that should be encouraged or avoided with adults?

There are some simple rules-of-thumb based on research, on experience and on common sense which can help give answers to all these problems. First, it is important to distinguish between 'teaching' and 'learning'. Sadly, you can be teaching away vigorously, but your students are not necessarily learning:

> I have never in my life found such terrible teaching as on the term's course of lectures we had on industrial law. For a start I couldn't see why supervisors had to do law anyway, but in any case we didn't learn any. I used to jot down a few notes, it was less boring than doing the *Mirror* crossword like some people did – I used to swear that the lecturer would never have noticed if the whole class had played noughts and crosses because once

> he'd started it would have taken an earthquake to stop him. His method was to introduce the week's topic, define it so quickly that the definition could have flown out of the window before you could take it in, say 'Any questions?' and then without waiting for the answer plod on in his usual loud deadpan voice for an hour and a half non-stop. It was completely remote from our actual work and if you did try to understand there were so many legal terms that you could never remember one from another. At the end of the lesson he gave us printed notes on what he'd been talking about – he was a conscientious chap really – but these only made it worse because they weren't at all the same as what he'd said in the lesson. His method of finding out if we'd understood was to suddenly spring a 'test' on us. Presumably he found out how we were doing but we never did, we never saw the papers again and he never gave us the marks, though we did ask. I'd been on a residential course where I'd learnt more in a few days than in a term at this place, so I knew it was all rubbish. I complained to the senior lecturer but it didn't do any good, the next day-release course had him, just the same.

Here was a teacher who had prepared conscientiously, who probably left his classroom exhausted by the draining effort of speaking for an hour and a half, but whose students had learnt nothing. Learning can only be accomplished by the learner. It is not only grammatically incorrect to say 'I learned him', it is a literal impossibility.

All learning is best done through active involvement. Imagine that you are a non-driver and that you want to learn how to drive. There are three methods open to you: to go to a lecture where a tutor tells you how to do it, to watch a skilled driver at work, or to practise in a real car with a teacher at your side. Would you have any hesitation about which method to choose? It is perfectly obvious that only the real practice would help you learn how to drive, although the other methods might conceivably give you some marginal help once you were on your way.

What is true for driving, a 'sensory motor skill', is equally true of every other kind of learning, whether it is 'cognitive' (that is, about knowledge) or 'behavioural' (a change in attitudes). The only effective way to learn is by *doing*.

There is one special reason why this is important for adult learners. As we grow older, our 'short-term' memory faculty becomes less efficient and more easily disturbed. What seems to happen is that our brains receive information and scan it for 'meaning' in order to 'decode' it at some future date. If this scanning stage is interrupted, the information never passes from short-term to long-term memory.

In everyday living we experience this as a minor nuisance: for instance, forgetting the telephone number while we look up the STD code. Where learning is concerned, any method that relies too much on short-term memory (for instance, lectures or demonstrations) is doomed to failure unless stringent measures are taken to prevent it. The reason is that the words of the lecturer or demonstrator are perceived by our brains as a never-ending series of information slabs. Each successive slab interferes with the 'storage' of its predecessor. The result is the phenomenon we all know: the feeling that we have been fed a mass of information, all of it undigested.

Ask yourself, as a test, what stick in your mind as the outstanding pieces of learning you accomplished at school and then, if you had higher education, at college or university. My guess is that you are unlikely to nominate sitting spellbound at the feet of a 'great teacher'. It is far more likely that you will immediately remember your part in a particular school play, a project, a trip abroad, an experiment you concluded on your own, the successful achievement of some sporting feat after months of trying – all of them active pieces of learning where you were in the centre of the effort. From three years' study of history at university, my mind has wiped most dates, wars, monarchs and all the essays and lectures that went into recording them. Asked by one son recently about when the Industrial Revolution started and by the other son why William of Normandy had invaded England in 1066, I could not give any coherent response to either. Yet I can still recall much of the detail of a project in my final year at university when, as a special privilege, and after much nagging of our tutors, we were allowed to research and write up a subject of our own choice. The other highlight was joining an archaeological 'dig' at a Romano-British site. I learnt more here in five days about the principles of archaeology than I had in two terms of academic study.

For learning to stick, it has to be 'internalized' – you have to make it your own. To achieve that, you must be actively involved in a series of tasks that lead you inexorably to the heart of the skill.

One of the best-researched pieces of 'proof' that active learning works best even for knowledge-based subjects is still the research done by Doctors Eunice and Meredith Belbin in the 1960s.* At that time British Rail had to turn its steam-locomotive drivers into people who understood electricity and could accomplish simple fault-finding on the diesel electric engines they would be driving. The organization's first attempts to train the drivers involved perfectly competent lectures on 'the principles of electricity'. These were a failure. The men sat politely through the classes and failed the end-of-course tests. The Belbins were brought in to solve the problem.

Instead of lectures, the Belbins designed a series of circuit boards. The trainees worked in pairs with three progressively more complicated sets of wooden boards. The first board carried a battery, an ammeter and a switch. Each pair was also given a bulb, a bulb holder, a more powerful battery, two small electric motors, and some wire and clips. Written instructions told them which pieces of apparatus to assemble with which, invited them to take away, add and experiment in various ways with the apparatus on the boards, then to observe and draw conclusions. This was the first part of the instruction sheet:

1 Look at the electrical circuit laid out on the board. It contains a battery, a bulb, a switch and an ammeter. Make sure you can see each of these things.
Starting at one side of the battery, the wire goes to the ammeter. It then goes to the ____, then to the ____, and then back to the ____.
Where does the needle point on the ammeter?____.
Press the switch down.
The ammeter needle now shows ____ amps.
The bulb____.
Now unclip the wire from one side of the battery and press the switch.
The ammeter needle now shows ____ amps.
The bulb ____.
Clip the wire back on the battery and press the switch again.
Does the bulb light now?____. What does the ammeter show?____.

* E. Belbin and M. Belbin, *Problems in Adult Retraining*, Heinemann, 1972.

> Now unclip the wire from the bulb and press the switch. What does the ammeter show?____.
> Does the bulb light?____.
> The current flows only if the switch is ____ and all the wires are ____.
> The circuit can be broken by unclipping a wire or by the ____.
> Switches are an easy way for us to break a ____ when we wish. But wires are usually ____ by accident. Either way, if the circuit is broken ____ happens.

In this way, instead of listening passively to an instructor who told them how a circuit works, or who drew it for them on the blackboard, the trainees actually constructed a circuit themselves. They saw through their own observed experience that an electrical circuit must have an undisturbed path before it can flow from one pole of the battery to the other. Instead of struggling with verbal explanations of a new word like 'ammeter', they saw for themselves and made use of the fact that it measured the flow of current. From these simple beginnings the trainees worked through this and two more boards, the last of which simulated the power circuit of a diesel electric locomotive.

During the sessions the instructor remained in the background, ready to answer questions, usually turning a question back to the questioner by inviting him to experiment further.

The results of this work were strikingly in favour of the active method. Not only did the trainees have higher scores on tests than those trained by conventional classroom teaching, they also did so in half the time. Differences between older and younger trainees disappeared: in fact on one test the older men in the 'active' group did much better than the younger men in the conventionally taught group.

The Belbins dubbed their method the 'discovery' method, a label which perhaps now seems a little quaint. Many developments in industry and education – not least open learning – have built on and overtaken the particularity of the technique. None the less, after twenty years, the Belbins' contribution to the wider theory of adult learning still seems immense because it revealed so clearly that the *process* (activity) matters more than the *subject*.

The same principles can be very widely applied, even to aesthetic subjects like stage design, in this case for a group of teachers interested in amateur drama production:

> The tutor did very little teaching as such. We spent all the available time doing things ourselves. This came as no particular surprise as we expected it to be practical. I suppose we did think we would be given some rules of thumb but none were promulgated at any time. Our first lessons were on basic elements of design. In the very first of these we arrived to find large pieces of paper and felt pens all laid out ready. Mr ___ explained that we were going to do an experiment to explore the relation between emotion and design. It had never occurred to most of us that there could be such a relation, and there were some scoffers! We were told how to divide our sheets into large grids and were then directed to the blackboard for further instructions. These were things like 'Draw horizontal lines an even distance apart', or 'Draw diagonal lines close together'. When we had done several of these we were asked to look carefully at each one and to write at the side, without conferring with our neighbours, what emotions or feelings each set of lines suggested. We could write several for each grid. When we then discussed our suggestions, it was extraordinary how much they agreed. Maybe one person had written 'peace' for the horizontal lines, another 'monotony' and another 'depression', but the basic idea of a low-key, quiet emotion was the same. We later did the same kind of thing with shape (cut-out black shapes on white paper) and colour. We had a lot of quite exciting discussions in these classes and found we were able to carry through the ideas easily into our later work on actual stage design.

In this course it is noticeable that there is no suggestion of an aesthetic 'right answer'. 'Depression' was accepted along with 'peace' as a reasonable individual reaction to a set of horizontal lines. The class evidently accepted the method itself with equanimity, and it seems that the task, though extremely simple and streamlined, was still challenging enough to have provoked all the excitement and interest one would expect where people are exploring for themselves rather than being told.

This learning, like the British Rail drivers' project, worked for a number of reasons that are fundamental to the success of any learning:

- it was preceded by a careful analysis of the skills needed;
- the learners were wholly and actively involved in their learning all the time;
- the learners were allowed to work at their own pace: an important topic in itself.

Pace

Imposing one pace on a group is not an effective way for the group to learn. Perhaps you vividly remember, as I do, the yawning boredom of schooldays where the main method of teaching was hour after hour of being talked *at* by the teacher. At my 'direct grant' school we were already 'creamed off' from our age-cohort but once there, we were ruthlessly streamed again. Even so, in any one class there were wide individual differences between our abilities. At gymnastics, my clumsiness and caution made me a slow learner, left far behind by nimbler friends; I struggled in the middle band in Physics and Chemistry. In some other subjects I was bored by waiting for others to catch up. If the pace is fixed to suit the fastest it will demotivate the majority; if it is right for the middle band it will alienate both the brighter and the slower learners.

This is why most schools, even those who grade and stream children, have settled for active methods of learning, like projects, 'supported self-study' and other resource-based techniques. Not, as has been sometimes been alleged, because competition is ideologically unsound, but because working at your own pace is far more *effective* (as long, of course, as the teacher is chasing you all the time to increase the quality and quantity of the work you do).

With adults this is especially important. The older you are, research has consistently shown, the more likely you are to want to sacrifice speed for accuracy in learning, and the more you are likely to want more information before making a response. Scores of different experiments have shown that if adults are asked to learn something new *under time pressure*, the older they are, the more likely they are to become confused and to make mistakes. Where no clock watching is involved, there is no difference in performance.

When no allowance is made for the increase in individual differences which age and experience bring, when the decline in short-term memory is ignored, and where teachers simply plunge on bearing the whole load of information-giving themselves, packing every moment with fresh and complex detail, then some classroom situations of monstrous futility and waste can develop:

> I came to nursing as a mature entrant, and I nearly left it for the same reason. I could not bear the monotony of sitting for hour after hour in an old-fashioned classroom where we were treated like children and where the 'facts' came at you in the same steady stream all the time. No attempt was made to involve us in the learning: the only thing that mattered was passing the exams. It was like a convent school full of silly adults!

In industry, training schools have found, literally to their cost, that set training periods of perhaps three weeks with formal tests at the end produce a high failure rate, even though sometimes the trainees have been offered an extra training period. Changing to a system where there is no set length of time for training, where assessment and not examination is employed, and where trainees come in at different times and not in batches, usually produces a consistently better success rate.

It follows that competition with one another and exhortations to 'keep up with the others' are not appropriate for adults because competition is only another way of introducing pacing. It is better for adults to measure their progress against their own previous performance rather than to attempt frantic rivalry with neighbours. This is easier said than done when so much of education is conducted on competitive lines (mark-lists with individual placing, prizes for best work, and so on) and when so much stress is put on speed and competition in work and social life. Michael Barratt Brown described the kind of outstanding contribution that can be made by so-called 'slow learners' when a totally uncompetitive and protective environment was established on their day-release courses:

> It needs to be said that tutors of trade-union classes soon learn that our society puts an enormous premium upon mental speed – quickness of grasp and response. This is part of the whole competitive environment in which we are brought up – in the home, at school, in the eleven-plus, in the labour market and at work. The quick thinker wins and the slow thinker is lost and may never catch up. Yet it is our experience that, given time and an uncompetitive environment, the greater advances, the most

> profound contributions, the real intellectual exercising comes as much from the slow ones as from the quick one. Again and again when philosophical questions are raised it is not the quick ones with the grammar-school and technical education but the slow plodders, grappling with the new ideas until they master them, who get to the heart of the matter.*

In a classroom where the tutor is expositor, demonstrator and star turn, it is only rarely possible to avoid a competitive or one-pace atmosphere. Where the emphasis changes to the tutor as resource-planner, the situation is very different. Active learning allows for the fact that people start with different kinds of knowledge and work at different speeds. Work in pairs, as individuals, or in small groups becomes a possibility. The tutor can spend time 'on call' as consultant, sorting out particular difficulties as they arise. If there are always new pieces of work prepared, the tutor can direct different students to start different tasks so that in any one classroom there might be several groups working simultaneously.

Active methods of learning are based on the importance to learners of understanding what they are doing. Tutors will occasionally say sourly of active methods that they cannot see the objection to telling people what to do, and that it is 'easier' and 'quicker' to give them a few rules. It is true that it is bound to be much easier for tutors to reel off rules or theories, but it is hardly ever easier for the learner. Learning involves first of all a slow grasp of a small part of a particular situation and only gradually a real understanding of general rules. Starting with the general rules may seem to cut corners, but it takes longer in the end.

Many teachers, especially in 'leisure' classes, have got away with expository methods for a long time because no one has tried to assess how much their classes have understood and to what extent they are able to apply what they have learnt. This is the crunch. You cannot be said to have learnt how to bake a cake if you do not know what has gone wrong when the cake collapses in the oven; painters will need to know not just how to mix colours but also why they achieve one particular colour with one particular mix of paints. Understanding in learning leads to flexibility; flexibility leads to versatility in skill and accomplishment.

* Michael Barratt Brown, *Adult Education for Industrial Workers*, NIAE, 1969.

Active learning where learners pace themselves undoubtedly has several advantages over more conventional classroom teaching. Because it avoids verbal instruction and demonstration, the learner does not have to make special efforts to memorize. People remember things most easily when they have been actively involved in them; by using active methods every student can be actively involved all the time. There are none of those periods of desperate concentration on what the tutor is saying or doing, followed, especially in people already tired from a day's work, by inevitable lapses of attention. There are no times when students need to scribble hasty notes which even they will read later with surprise. There is no need for students to feel that, apart from the few moments of private attention they receive from the tutor, they might just as well be sitting at home.

Relevance

While of course there are people who are drawn to 'learning for learning's sake', most adult learners are strongly motivated by wishing to acquire skill and knowledge that they can use in immediate and practical ways.

As a tutor, the nearer you can make the learning to the 'real' world, the more acceptable it will be and therefore the more quickly and effectively your students will learn. The obverse is true, too: offer adults learning that they consider irrelevant and they may well become sulky and 'difficult'.

> I'm afraid I became a not-very-enthusiastic student in the latter stages of my Accountancy training. I had study leave and took some of it at a summer school. By then I had been actually working in accountancy for about four years, and so much of what we were taught at the School was purely about how to pass the exams: it had sweet FA to do with the skills I knew you needed for the job. Even though I knew I *had* to pass the exam because I and my firm had invested so much in me, I was aware of constantly interrupting the lecturers to challenge them about the practical benefits of what they were 'teaching' us.

> I was teaching a YTS group in the retail area. I very quickly realized that it was absolutely no good 'insulting' them with tasks they regarded as 'schooley' and irrelevant to their job

> placements. I tried to get them to do things like designing safety posters or fire instruction leaflets but this was a total failure. They knew that they would never in the foreseeable future have such responsibility 'for real'. Instead, it was much better to get them to do an assessment of safety policy and practice in their shop and to write it up. By doing that, they engaged in the real world with all its falling-short of the ideal and began to think about why that might be. The most popular parts of the course were always things like how to write out credit card vouchers correctly: they recognized that they were skills they badly needed to perform well in the placement with the hope that the employer would offer them something permanent at the end of it.

Exactly the same principles applied to craft teaching in adult education. Students who want to be able to service their cars are not likely to be interested in the history of the petrol engine; people who want to learn enough Spanish to be understood by shop assistants in Spain will not want to study nineteenth-century Spanish literature.

If you are involved in vocational training then your skill must be to make the training closely resemble the real task, even if some of the distractions and complications of the 'real' world have to be stripped away to lay bare the skeleton of the skill:

> I wasn't sure how far you could 'learn' negotiating, but I went along. It was excellent because all the exercises were based on *exactly* the sort of situations were encounter every day. We started with simple two-handers which we video-recorded then analysed, then we went on to more elaborate scenarios using the same principles, then working up to team-exercises. Some people felt it was 'artificial' because you didn't have all the business of personal histories of animosity etc. etc., but I felt that was a help: it allowed me to see the principles pretty clearly.

The rule holds good for any adult teaching, even when it is for those students whose intellectual abilities are far below the norm. One tutor of hospitalized mentally handicapped adults reported their indignation at having to practice handling money by using cardboard coins. She was forgiven for this blunder only when the rightly despised cardboard was replaced with the real thing.

The fact that so much vocational training in the past has ignored the need for realism and relevance and has therefore been rejected by employers and employees alike is one of the main reasons for the development of the National Council for Vocational Qualifications (NCVQ, see page 6). In future, a national vocational qualification (NVQ) will mean that only the skills needed for the job will count for testing. The foundation of the skill needed to do the job is 'competence', and qualification will be based on 'competencies', and competencies alone. Eventually even the professions will have to fall into line, even though most professional qualifications are heavily biased towards knowledge rather than skill, the medical profession notoriously so. Doctors do not have to be trained and to demonstrate skill in counselling, for instance, to qualify as doctors, even though skill in counselling is fundamental to good performance in the job.

A few years ago, I was involved in a small tussle which shows how strong the grip of traditional knowledge can be and how difficult it is to shake free from it. As a producer I was responsible for the BBC series *Save a Life*, which was about how to give emergency resuscitation. I offered with a small group of medical experts to write the pamphlet that would be available, free, to members of the public. Traditionally, all first aid manuals begin their instruction on resuscitation with a description of how the lungs work. There is usually a colour drawing showing the heart and lungs and a description of the exchange of oxygen. Sticking to my own principle of only including relevant material, my draft excluded all reference to this process. I felt that knowing how the lungs worked was not necessary in order to revive an apparently 'dead' person and that the usual drawing of red and blue 'pipes' and 'sponges' was a distraction from the job of learning the life-saving routine. This departure from tradition was stoutly resisted over many hours of argument by many of the doctors on our main advisory group and if we had not been vigorously supported by some influential younger doctors, I doubt that we would have had our way.

So the lesson of 'relevance' is that it relates back both to motivation and to a careful skills analysis. You assume that students are in your group because there is a practical skill relating to the 'outside world' that they wish to acquire. This skill must be analysed and broken down, then translated into material that the learner will immediately recognize for its relevance to the task:

> My company is involved in exporting to Germany, Austria and Switzerland and I decided I must learn some German. My first attempts were hopeless because all the books and tapes I tried were full of tourist stuff about booking double beds. I eventually found a wonderful open learning course which had exactly what I needed. Not only did it include masses of vocabulary (just right for business people), it also gave plenty of down to earth advice on how not to put your foot in it culturally!

Reinforcement and practice

Ideally, as a tutor you will break down the skill you are teaching into small sections, each easily understood, and each leading logically to the next.

> The company puts 'customer care' high on its list of priorities and my job is to help train our assistants. We start with why customer care matters, go onto how to welcome customers, then how to give information, then how to handle complaints. The skills the trainees learn in the first session (eye contact, 'positive' body language, smiling, attentiveness) are used over and over again in the rest of the course. You can't learn how to handle a complaint correctly if you haven't learnt the basic body-language message, so we concentrate on it in the very first session.

Approaching the subject in this way has various virtues. First, learners see for themselves that the course has a logical structure and that each section leads to the next. This is especially appealing to adults. We are not daunted by seeing the whole spread of a syllabus laid out before us. But perhaps more importantly, a well-designed course will always oblige students to go on 'reinforcing' skills and knowledge learnt earlier. Without reinforcement, the skill will fade. I referred earlier to the 'Save a Life' campaign, where in the course of the campaign many tens of thousands of people learned the basic techniques of cardiopulmonary resuscitation by going to a special two-hour class. Even now that the campaign is officially over, the work continues in many towns and cities. Each class is constructed so that everyone starts by learning to open the airway in an unconscious person, then to give mouth-to-mouth ventilation (the 'kiss of life') and then chest compressions ('heart message'). All these techniques are taught in a sequence which becomes progressively more complex, but each 'practice' involves using again the techniques acquired earlier. So, for instance, you never *just* practice chest compressions, you always go through the whole sequence so that in the process of practising giving compressions you are also reinforcing what you have learnt about opening the airway.

However, even with the best teaching, American research has shown how quickly this skill fades. Without reinforcement, many people forget vital parts of the sequence after about six months. For this reason, if you are qualified to give first aid at work, you can only hold your certificate for a maximum of three years. After that you must go on a refresher course.

The same principles of practice and reinforcement apply to every subject. An advanced language student will need to apply the simple vocabulary and structures acquired in the first few days of the course. In embroidery, the simple stitches, fortunately, are the basis of all the more elaborate ones. In subjects like these, the reinforcement comes naturally; in others you will need to apply more guile.

Using experience

The best-designed adult learning aims to build on all the advantages and minimize the disadvantage of the rich experience adults bring with them.

Earlier in this century, trainers and teachers alike tended to bemoan the fact that adults were not the nice blank sheet apparently presented by children. Previous experience in adult learners was seen as a chronic disadvantage, making students 'slow'. Looking back now, perhaps it is easier to see that the 'slowness' was most probably a natural resistance to peremptory and authoritarian methods of teaching rather than a devastating handicap which inevitably creeps on with age.

As adults we have experience of the world and probably also some experience of the subject we have enrolled to learn. For this reason we will usually have a great deal to contribute, even if we are also much more likely to be sceptical and challenging of 'rules':

> My most enjoyable classes have always been with the mature women students who want to take up teaching after rearing their

> families. They simply will not accept pat theories and glib statements about child development because all the time they are asking 'Did my children do that?' Or 'Was that true when my children were four?' Whereas a twenty-year-old will write it straight down in her notebook, the mature woman always pauses to weigh and consider against her own and other people's experience. She always sees the 'ifs' and 'buts'. In these classes, by relating the student's experience to the general view, I feel we finally create a tremendously lively and complex picture of child psychology. They bring a depth and humour to rather dry theories which young people could never attain.

This polytechnic tutor found that her experience of teaching mature students was rewarding precisely because they did challenge and argue. Unfortunately, the same phenomenon can be deeply unsettling if you are less secure, or perhaps simply unused to it:

> I moved into adult retraining schemes after several years' teaching in secondary schools where I had been responsible for Careers Advice. The first six months was very hard going. I found I had to reappraise my ideas about how to teach. Take the topic of looking for a job, for instance. At school I used to give the pupils simple rules about how to dress for an interview, how to behave when being interviewed and so on. I found the adults either just sat there stolidly and didn't react at all, or else constantly interrupted, rather rudely actually, and told me that I didn't know anything about it. I had a job, I'd never been unemployed so what right had I got to advise them? In their experience, interviewers didn't behave in the way I'd suggested . . . What I was saying was all nonsense . . . I knew it wasn't all nonsense and that they did need my help. The penny dropped when I sat in with a colleague and saw how she didn't make 'statements' or lay down the law. She opened up the topic, asked for opinions and experiences and drew the 'advice' out of that. It's much harder to do this than I'd thought and it took me probably another 3–4 months to learn to do the same.

It is essential, then, to solicit and 'use' the experience of your learners. Failing to do so risks rejection of your message. More positively, by inviting comment, you eventually arrive at a much richer and denser picture of the world, and one that is therefore more relevant to real life. The more students are involved by offering their own experience, the more they are likely to 'internalize' the learning.

This involvement is important for another reason. Suppose you encounter the 'downside' of adult experience: the stubbornly entrenched view, the commitment to one particular technique even if it is incorrect, the hidden gap in knowledge. How are you to counter these 'mistakes' if you don't know what they are? How will students ever learn 'better' if they are never obliged to hold existing experience to the light so that they see the holes in it for themselves?

'Arousal'

As adult learners we are more experienced and world-weary, and we also come to classes needing a good jolt to the system before we can start learning. This will be particularly true of groups meeting in the evenings, but it can apply just as much to daytime courses. Most of us will be preoccupied, often still half-thinking about other responsibilities, and in the evenings simply tired. For this reason an intensely involving initial ten-minutes is always a good idea:

> Five minutes of warm-up exercises – gets everyone in the mood – shakes off the cares of the day.
>
> *Aerobics teacher, sports centre*

> A controversial bit of video . . . or a five-minute audio tape, followed by brisk discussion.
>
> *Politics tutor, polytechnic*

> Swim two lengths, to a fast time limit. That gets them going!
>
> *Swimming tutor, local authority pool*

> Seven minutes of mental arithmetic . . . fast and fun. Perks everybody up.
>
> *GCSE Maths tutor*

> Icebreaker exercises designed to help people get to know each other and also to relax.
>
> *'Team-building' management consultant*

Such techniques are successful for these tutors because they have certain elements in common, vital to the success of any opening session with adults:

- everyone in the group takes part;
- to do them at all you must be involved;
- they are fun.

Learning to learn

Finally, can adults 'learn to learn'? All the evidence suggests that the answer is 'yes'. First, experience of learning improves performance. Students who have kept mentally in trim by maintaining a consistent 'diet' of learning from time to time tend to do better than otherwise identical students who have not. The reasons seem partly to do with practice, and partly to do with self-confidence.

But even where there has been no adult practice at learning, you can improve the performance of your learners by helping them 'learn to learn'. It will probably be vital to do this in any course which is designed to last longer than a week, where testing and assessment are part of the outcome of the course. Where the group largely consists of people who have not been involved in formal learning since leaving school, some simple, well-designed help in rapid-reading, note-taking, memorizing, essay or project writing and assessment techniques can often produce sensational improvements in a short time. If you are teaching this kind of group, it may well be worth building such help into the early stages of the syllabus.

Checklist on learning

Are your students actively involved in their learning throughout most of the sessions? ☐

Are you avoiding techniques, such as lectures and demonstrations, which create short-term memory problems? ☐

Are your learners working at their own pace? ☐

Is competition explicitly discouraged? ☐

Is the learning relevant to the skills and knowledge needed to perform well in the subject, especially in the 'real' situation outside the class? ☐

Do you build in frequent opportunities for reinforcement and practice? ☐

Do you constantly solicit and 'use' the experience of the students? ☐

Are the first few minutes of the class always attention-grabbing? ☐

4

Giving feedback

The old saying that practice makes perfect is not true. But it is true to say that it is practice the *results of which are known* which makes perfect.

F. C. Bartlett *

Giving 'feedback' and criticism, praising and commenting, these are all so important in learning that the topic deserves a whole chapter to itself. Teaching adults is complicated enormously by the difficulty of 'criticizing' an equal. Not giving the right quantity or quality of feedback is one of the main reasons why adult learning fails, so it is worth thinking about how to get it right. Basically, there are two dangers: giving it in the wrong way and not giving enough.

> I went to a two day workshop on how to give presentations. I was one of only two women so I felt conspicuous anyway. It was run by a management training consultant, but 'in-house'. I gave my first little presentation and I knew it was bad – I was so nervous I could hardly speak. The trainer's comments were devastating. I was utterly destroyed. I'm afraid I broke down and cried. The next day I just could not bring myself to go in to work so I missed the second day. The whole thing was so mortifying it makes me cringe now to think of it. I learnt nothing; my terror of speaking in public was worse than it had ever been and my credibility with my bosses took a long time to recover.

> My first experience of learning as an adult was a complete damp squib. I'd enrolled for a jewellery class at a very good London Institute. The tutor was a well-known craftsman but had no experience of teaching. He was a good demonstrator, but nothing more. I slaved over my little projects, but I never got a

* F. C. Bartlett, 'The measurement of human skill', *British Medical Journal*, vol. 1, 1947.

> *crumb* of comment from him. He'd look at my efforts and would just say 'Hmmmm . . . yes' and pass on. What did this 'Hmmm . . . yes' mean? 'Awful'? 'OK'? 'Boring?' 'Beneath contempt'? I never found out! I went on going to the class because the facilities were wonderful and the other students very friendly. We helped each other, but it would have been so much better to have had comment from him.

Feedback matters, because without it the learner is unlikely to improve. Imagine that you are one member of a group whose task is to throw a ball over your shoulders at a target. Your group does not receive any guidance on whether the balls are hitting the target. There is another group which does receive guidance. Who is most likely to hit the target most often? Your group is going to continue haphazardly making the same errors over and over again. The other group will steadily improve. This simple and classic experiment has actually been performed and the results showed over and over again that, without feedback, performance cannot improve.

If performance does not improve, then all learners, but particularly adults, quickly lose interest: their motivation flags, and without motivation there can be no learning. Adults are rarely obliged to continue with a learning project against their will. By the time we have reached adulthood most of us are adept at slithering away from situations where we feel we perform badly.

Good feedback is one of the basic rewards of learning and is therefore a critical part of the learning cycle which goes like this:

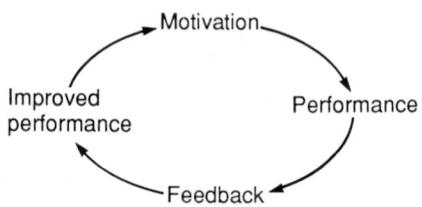

If as a tutor you break this cycle by failing to give the right kind of feedback then the learning will fail – as happened in 'presentation workshop' quoted earlier. What is especially sad about this example is that the learner blamed herself, whereas in fact the failure was the tutor's.

To put it more positively, the sensational effect of just a little well-judged feedback can surprise even an experienced tutor:

> Although I was an OU tutor for many years, it never failed to amaze me what effect my comments had. It was quite common for students to ring me after they'd had their TMAs (Tutor-Marked Assignments) back and to say things like 'You've no idea how many times I've read what you said'; 'I felt *thrilled* that you'd given me that mark'; 'I was thinking of giving up, but you've encouraged me so much I'm going to carry on'. Often I'd only written about 15 lines, but it was enough to make all the difference to a student who'd been wondering whether to give up or not.

There is one other reason for taking feedback especially seriously with adult learners. It seems that once a mistake has been made, it is far more likely to be repeated over and over again than with a young learner. Adults seems to find it harder to recognize that they have made a mistake, and harder to 'unlearn' it. Hence the importance of immediately giving feedback.

This difficulty can be compounded when the problem is not only to correct errors made on the spot, but to discover what basic misunderstandings from the past may still be hindering a student's progress. It would be commonplace, for instance, for an English teacher to find that students who demand 'grammar' have no idea of what 'parts of speech' are. They have never learnt that words can be classified in this way.

The industrial psychologist, Meredith Belbin, has commented on how, in industrial training, individuals may struggle to disguise their lack of knowledge of basic measurement. He says that, on asking some trainees how many sixteenths they thought there were in an inch, one trainee said 'ten' and another one said 'twelve'. Correctly identifying mistaken assumptions from the past is sometimes so important that absolutely no progress can be made until it is done. Much of the skill in teaching adult non-readers, for instance, lies in finding out exactly what it is in their past which has prevented them from learning to read. Sometimes the cause might be simple failure to learn the eccentric rules of English spelling. More frequently, there is a combination of mechanical and psychological reasons.

It seems from research that once mistakes have been made it is particularly hard to correct them and that the solution seems to be prevention rather than cure. Prevention in this case means making absolutely sure that on the first occasion of a new piece of learning the adult gets the right answer. This first occasion seems to be the really crucial one and mistakes made then are peculiarly hard to eradicate. Devising tasks where 'right first time' responses are highly likely is the best solution, but standing by to give feedback is certainly the next best line of defence.

When to give feedback

There is a simple rule about the optimum time to give feedback on learning: *give it as soon as possible.* Don't wait until either the triumph or the error is repeated. Give it immediately. The reason is that learning is like quick-drying paint. You only have a short time to correct the mistake or let it harden into a permanent error. If something is wrong, then put it right straight away. If all is well, then say so and say why and the learner can speed on to the next stage. If there is a mistake, help the learner put it right on the spot. The best time to give comment is while the effort of making the attempt is still fresh and the 'arousal' effect is still there. Leave it until later and learners may have settled back into complacency, or into an environment – home, for instance – where your influence is more easily resisted.

> I was sent on a supervisory management course – only a few days – by my company when I had just been promoted. I thought it was quite interesting and moderately helpful and that I'd done all right. Imagine my dismay when *six weeks later* I was handed a copy of a report from the trainer to my line manager saying that he thought I needed a great deal more training in certain aspects – for instance running meetings and writing business letters. I'd thought I was doing quite well. I was furious. Why on earth hadn't something been said at the time? By that time I was well into the job anyway, and my basic attitude was '____ you! I don't need training anyway!' Much, much later on, I realized that I didn't know anything like as much as I'd thought, but the opportunity to learn quickly had most definitely been missed.

How to give feedback

Here we come to the heart of the skill of teaching adults. As a tutor you are the peer of your students. Indeed many of your students may, in their non-student roles, be the kind of people who may rightly make you feel humble. You cannot rely on being their 'superior' in age, income, social class or occupation, only in your knowledge of your subject. Because of this, it is your right and your duty to comment on their efforts. The problem is how to do it effectively while leaving them with their dignity intact.

It is often said that 'we learn by our mistakes'. I have often thought how thoroughly misleading this statement is. It would seem truer to say that we learn by our successes, *as long as we know why we are being successful*. First, we have to accept that as human beings our craving for praise and reassurance is utterly limitless. Praise makes us feel secure and confident, where negative criticism makes us insecure and self-doubting. But we can only learn from praise when we know what we are being praised for. Let's return to the example of the ball thrown over the shoulder at a target. Suppose you achieve a bull's eye and your 'tutor' says only 'yes, you hit the centre'. Would you know for sure what it was in your performance which achieved the result? I should say that this was unlikely. By contrast, your tutor might say 'Yes, good! You hit the bull. The reason was that you flicked your wrist to the right just as your hand reached shoulder level'. This feedback is much more likely to help you repeat your success, for three reasons:

- it is given promptly;
- it contains the encouraging word 'good' – your tutor sounds pleased at your achievement;
- it gives detailed comment on *how* you achieved an accurate result.

Giving learners reasons for their success or failure is thus one absolutely fundamental rule for helpful feedback. Don't just say 'That was a good piece of work', or 'Well done'. Always give the reason: 'That was excellent because it was so neat', or 'Good – you looked confident, your nerves were under control and your voice was at just the right level'. However, for feedback to stick and to be even more effective, this process has to be two-way.

> As a managing agent for YTS I see a number of people who are not formally trained 'tutors' doing brilliant jobs. There's one chap who is superb: he is a good craftsman himself, but his trainees produce beautiful work in what seems like a very short time. When I watched him I realized that this is because all the comment on their work is a *dialogue*. First he sets the standard by showing them what perfect bricklaying or carpentry looks like, and he even produces some 'shoddy' examples for comparison. Then he takes each trainee's effort and discusses it with them so that they are spotting for themselves what the problems and good points are, and how they happened, and then they are pointed to finding a way for themselves of putting it right.

This mixture of gentleness and ruthlessness can be difficult to achieve. It is pointless to put all the onus on the hapless student by demanding brusquely, 'Now what was wrong with that?' Many students will babble on guiltily in such circumstances without any real idea of the justice of their self-accusations. It is far better to establish a constructive dialogue which helps students compare their own performance with the ideal and which helps them diagnose strengths and weakness for themselves. This puts responsibility where it belongs: on the learner, not the teacher.

It is usually best, too, to concentrate on only a few aspects of performance, whether good or bad. There is a limit to what most of us can absorb at a time without either intellectual overload or (if we are being criticized) damaged self-esteem.

> I was a tutor on a literacy scheme. I discovered early on that marking every single error in the writing was totally counterproductive: the students just couldn't take it, it was too dispiriting. Instead, I concentrated on about three significant mistakes each time. The improvement was usually staggering.

As well as concentrating on just a few mistakes at a time, try to make your feedback unambiguous and clear. In an effort to avoid being 'hurtful' some tutors wrap up their comments in so many layers of qualification or anecdote that the main point is obscure. It is better to say straightforwardly what the problem is, to give the reason, and to leave it there. For instance, suppose you are training a young person in how to write a memo. Your trainee produces a reasonable effort, but it is too long. Your feedback is best delivered as some warm words of praise for whatever has been done well, and then a few succinct sentences saying that the draft is too long and why. You should avoid garlanding your comments with anecdotes about your own first efforts to write memos, funny memos you have seen in the past, or office gossip about the addressee. Enjoyable though this may be, especially for you, it will obscure the impact of your feedback.

There is one other common temptation which you should resist. If you see a mistake, don't march in, pick up the work and 'put it right' by doing a large amount of it yourself. As the expert, you know how to do it; it is the students who have to learn by doing it themselves.

Some teachers who rightly pride themselves on the standard of their own work, sometimes find their students' mistakes too painful to contemplate, and will often seize the work and do the difficult bits themselves, sometimes under the impression that students are grateful for such professional additions. There may be occasional students too placid to object, but most people feel cheated if someone else does all the hard work for them. They want the satisfaction and sense of achievement of learning to cope for themselves. They may find the tutor's well-meant interventions hard to endure, as in this art class run by a teacher whom the student earlier described tactfully as having 'tremendous enthusiasm but lacking method'.

> General instruction is given *ad hoc* . . . moreover, in dealing with someone's problem, his enthusiasm leads him to paint half the picture himself, instead of merely demonstrating and suggesting and thereby letting the student feel that the picture was 'all his own work'. This makes everyone cross, but no one has had the courage to tell him we don't like it.

It is also better to leave the student to work out the solution: you can suggest that the memo might be too long, but the details of how to achieve a better length should be up to the student. Prescriptive feedback only postpones the problem to another occasion because it is your solution not the learner's.

There are various other kinds of unhelpful feedback. One is the sort that is so generalized or vague that it leaves the learner completely stumped: 'You should try to be a bit more assertive . . .', or 'Your work lacks dynamism . . .', or 'It would be better if there were more light and shade in your performance'. All these are vague, waffly statements capable of dozens of different interpretations and quite unlikely to result in improved performance. Then there is the feedback that appears completely subjective: 'I don't like the way you paint clouds', or 'I prefer a different kind of analysis myself'. Learners will be much more likely to reject such comments as personal prejudice than if they are rephrased more objectively: 'There are lots of other ways to paint clouds . . . one of them is . . .'.

Another trap is to offer feedback on aspects of performance that people are simply unlikely to be able to improve because of circumstance or fundamental personality: for instance criticizing a woman javelin thrower for not having the same powerful arm action as a man, or telling someone that his accent is difficult to understand. Whatever feedback you offer, it should always be possible for the learner to act on it.

One principle is fundamental to the whole idea of constructive feedback: criticize the performance, not the person. All good tutors convey their liking and respect for their students and their longing for them to improve. This is the quality in good teachers that is most essential for success, hardest to pinpoint and impossible to counterfeit, but we all know it when we see it:

> He just burnt with a wish for us to know what he knew . . . we *knew* we were the best class he'd ever taken and yet all his classes felt like that . . . We all knew that we individually were the students he cared about . . . and yet we knew he had no favourites!

> It was an extremely supportive atmosphere: very caring, very friendly, yet she was utterly ruthless with us. Sloppy effort was not allowed, the words 'I can't' were banned. Whatever criticisms were made, they were made knowing that she really urged you towards improvement and achievement because she liked you and had faith in you.

I once had the opportunity as a learner myself to compare two tutors teaching rather similar courses at the BBC. The first tutor, whom I shall call 'John' had on paper a textbook-correct course. The objectives were clear, the curriculum looked interesting and perfectly paced. 'Andrew's' course looked, and was, hectic, competitive and over-full. Yet students ended John's course rebellious, unhappy and disappointed by the small amount achieved. There were even rumours of fisticuffs. Andrew's students, by contrast, gave him an end-of-course champagne party and forgave him the torment he had caused us by piling on work and stress. Why was this? The answer seems clear. John's course, for all its apparent perfection, was marred by his biting, sarcastic comments on our work, by his inability to remember our names or departments from one session to the next and by his refusal ever to offer praise. Andrew's comments on the other hand, though often severe, were never hurtful. He would recall our improvement from previous exercises, showed he never forgot our backgrounds, would offer praise for achievement, looked us in the eye, smiled, nodded encouragement and cheered our little successes. Even now, twelve years on, I still think of him warmly and feel grateful for the rigorous technical standards I acquired, thanks to him.

One aspect of Andrew's technique holds good for any tutor: always offer some praise and offer it before the negative comments. However poor the performance, there must be some aspect which is praiseworthy.

> Our pottery teacher was wonderful. He used to call us together two or three times in the course of the class and say 'Look everyone, we all *must* see so-and-so's pot – it's so terrific – see the subtle glaze (or the slip, or the way the handle was put on). Isn't it *wonderful*! Just a teeny problem with the shape here – that's because of problems with X or Y – but *very* exciting!' I thought this was very clever. So-and-so glowed at the attention, learnt from mistakes, high standards were established, and a terrifically companionable atmosphere emerged. Somehow, by lucky chance, everyone's work achieved this spotlight over the course of the term!

Where a class combines commitment to high standards with a friendly, non-competitive atmosphere, another benefit emerges: students will begin to offer constructive and useful feedback to each other because they are following the example set by the tutor. It may even be possible to arrange exercises where they specifically do so by working in pairs and offering feedback to each other.

Although 'public' feedback can be useful with a secure and friendly group, in general it is safer, certainly at first, to give feedback privately. Comments on essays should be written for that learner's eyes only; thoughts on how to improve a skill are best delivered one-to-one and without eavesdroppers.

All feedback sessions should end with a mutually agreed summary of what is to be done to overcome mistakes and build on successes. In the training sessions I run myself, I like the 'action plan' idea as an effective way both of rounding off a session and of pointing to the future. Rather than encourage a euphoric (and I'm afraid often pointless) 'evaluation', I will hand each participant a blank 'Personal Action Plan'. This will include spaces to write a personal evaluation under headings such as 'skills in which I already feel reasonably confident given my training and experience', 'skills in which I have made progress during this course' and 'skills in which I need more practice', followed by a list of ways in which further training or practice could be achieved, with target dates for completion.

Another way of achieving the same end would be to arrange a brief meeting to agree a couple of action points which would include further practice in areas of weakness.

The point of techniques like this is to make sure that the feedback has been heard, understood, and will be acted on in the future. It is easy to forget that what you think is crystal clear may not always be understood by the learner:

> I went to a residential weekend on photography. The setting was beautiful, the food excellent, the other students fun, but I didn't learn much. It was most frustrating. The tutor was eager to give me comments on my efforts, but he was in another sphere with '*f*/this' and 'aperture-that' – it was all just a muddle in my mind. He would end by saying 'OK? Is that clear?' I'd just nod – I couldn't bear to say that it wasn't clear at all – I'd have felt even more of a fool. Then at the next session of course he'd look exasperated because I'd made the same mistake again and would say 'But I explained all this to you before!'

So giving feedback demands skill as well as tact. The secret of making sure that the message has been 'heard' is to ask open-ended questions like 'Now, just to make sure you've understood, you explain it all back to me', or 'Would you like to summarize what you think we've agreed?' or 'How are you planning to put all this into effect?'

Avoid closed questions which invite the answer 'yes' or 'no' – for instance 'Have you understood?' or 'Is that all right?' Closed questions do nothing to test whether the learner has really absorbed the feedback you have given. Look instead, for questions beginning 'Tell me', 'How' or 'Why'.

Finally, be generous with the overall amount of feedback you offer. Most teachers, in common with most managers, grossly overestimate the quantity of feedback they give. I once worked with a man who was notorious for reducing trainees (men and women) to tears of rage, frustration and humiliation. One of the reasons was his refusal (or inability perhaps) to give them feedback other than the occasional highly critical comment on their work. When tackled about this he looked at me in genuinely blank innocence. 'Surely they know', he said, 'that if I don't say anything, I must approve . . . and that even if I do have a criticism, I'm giving them nine out of ten?' Alas, the opposite was true. The few comments he did make were assumed to represent dozens of silent criticisms held back only by intense restraint and dislike of 'scenes'. Some of the young trainees he actually held in highest esteem were the very people who believed he thought little of their work.

To avoid misunderstandings of this sort, the guiding principle is that in every teaching session you should find ways to offer every learner some feedback. This may simply be through a self-checklist in a book, a how-did-you-do conversation with a partner, a private or public brief discussion on performance, written comments on an essay, an action plan for further training or a semi-formal session on general progress.

In giving feedback to learners your own skill as a tutor is severely tested. The possibilities for misunderstanding are endless, the risk of being hurtful or seeming personal ever-present, the temptation to say nothing, or to say too much, ever-looming. But without feedback, your learners cannot learn and as a tutor you cannot be said to be 'teaching'.

Checklist on feedback

Do you use several different methods of offering feedback to learners?

- written comment? ☐
- general progress discussion? ☐

comment on each 'performance'? ☐

action plans? ☐

Does every learner receive feedback during each session? ☐

Do you always give feedback immediately? ☐

Do you always praise the good points before criticizing the bad? ☐

Do you criticize the performance not the person? ☐

Do you always give *reasons* for your feedback? ☐

Do you check that the learner has understood the feedback by asking open-ended questions? ☐

Do you concentrate on just a few criticisms at a time? ☐

Do you create an atmosphere where students can give constructive feedback to each other? ☐

5

Understanding your group

Your students often don't realize that you are as nervous as they are – perhaps that's just as well!

OU Summer school tutor

My company does 'open access' workshops on key management skills. These workshops are very expensive for the learners or their companies; the group usually consists of ten nervous or sceptical individuals: they *know* what it's costing in fees let alone in opportunity costs to their companies while they are away from base. This puts me under considerable pressure to *deliver*. The result is that even after several years of experience, plus knowing that what we do is excellent and well-proven, I never start a new course without 'nerves'.

Management consultant

One's dread is that someone in the group will be more 'expert' than oneself! Or that they might refuse to try some of the projects . . . or that there will be subtle undermining of one's leadership . . . it's all possible. Fortunately, it rarely happens, but the mere thought is enough to give some quivers of apprehension before one starts.

Training officer, petroleum industry

This chapter is about tutors and their groups: how do learning groups behave? What teaching styles work best?

Anxieties

As the quotes at the beginning of this chapter show, worries about learning are not confined to learners. All teachers worth their salt feel some apprehension before beginning a new course. Will you know enough about your subject? Will your material last for the appropriate time? Will the students like you? Will the teaching you have planned be at the right level for the group? What if some of them drop out?

Schoolteachers who also teach adults often find this a particularly pressing problem. In school a teacher may feel no uncertainty about how to behave with the children. Schoolteachers are always older than their pupils, have the advantage of a longer education and can lean heavily on an established authority structure and tradition which is familiar to everyone. Even a sixth-form teacher faced with an unusually bright and mature set of pupils can take some comfort in longer and 'superior' experience. Not so teachers of adults. They may be younger than all their students, and may even be less intelligent; there is no familiar system or tradition to work in; they may be totally isolated from colleagues. They may have had no training whatever in teaching; the only distinguishing mark between themselves and their students may be their particular expertise in their subjects.

The tutor's influence

It is absolutely correct to have some worries about a new course group, but both the problem and the solution are in your own hands. Your influence is the most important single element in setting the style of a class; as great or even a greater influence on the whole occasion than the sum of all the other individuals. This will come as no surprise to experienced teachers, who will have noticed with dismay how even with a group of apparently stable and self-possessed adults who contribute a good deal to an active discussion, their own moods of exhilaration, pleasure, boredom or irritation are invariably conveyed to a class, and that these reflections from their own personality are in some degree returned as mirror images in the way students behave to them and to each other.

Compare, for instance, the atmosphere in the classroom and the response by students in two highly contrasted classes in the same institute. The groups were observed and then described in a report by the former principal of the institute, Ivy Cooper Marsh.

> *The French class* (students all roughly the same age, in their early 30s). He is a conscientious and knowledgeable man and, if he were not so rigid and traditional in his methods, his classes would be more enjoyable for the students and he would be able to keep the interests of a wider range of ages and abilities. This tutor is clearly not a tutor to meet the challenge of heterogeneity. He tends to use 'school' methods and to expect students to

learn by rote, a routine adults find unacceptable . . . Everything stems from the teacher and even when he was encouraged to have a circle of chairs, the tutor continued to keep the atmosphere formal. The activity of the student is boringly the same – repetition of words and phrases. The students admire him but find him formidable in spite of his good nature . . . There is no feeling in his classes of a group of adults engaged in a common project, and no incentive to widen horizons and learn to manage on their own when class attendance ceases, as it must at some time.

This tutor has repeatedly deplored the fact that without examinations you cannot get good standards or measure what you have done.

The fishing-rod-making class (students of widely varying ages). It would seem to be an excellent example of an unobtrusive teacher nevertheless emanating an atmosphere of competence, confidence and enthusiasm which produces in the learners the maximum effect and group goodwill . . .

He is a quiet man and there is absolutely no obvious domination of the class – indeed going into the workshop it is difficult to pick out the tutor – there are groups here and there discussing their work and helping one another. There is a feeling of interest and industry in the class generally and the atmosphere is relaxed. Any one of the students was willing to talk about what his neighbour was doing . . . most students coming to this class know what they want to do but the teacher is constantly showing them new materials and new methods. He has his own retail business and himself keeps abreast of innovations. In this manner he is authoritative on his subject – also a skilful craftsman himself – his students admire and respect his expertise. He has a wide interest around his craft and gives his students every benefit of this. Very old rods, which occasionally come his way, he brings in for his students to make comparisons with new types, and I have seen some old worthwhile rods being beautifully repaired and renovated by students in this class. In this way he is teaching his students to recognise good materials and expert workmanship and to admire and emulate such things.*

* Ivy Cooper Marsh, 'Adult students: an inquiry into how and why they learn', Eltham Adult Education Institute, 1969.

Even allowing for the differences in subject and students and for the personal preferences of the observer, it is clear that very different teaching styles were being used. In consequence the results each teacher was likely to achieve were deeply affected. The French teacher's formidable and rigorous drilling appealed to the highly motivated, fairly able students. The others (about half the initial enrolment) dropped out early in the term. Everything about this teacher's style emphasized the students' dependence on him; he was the sole source of information, and it is perhaps significant that he used no audio-visual aids (apart from a textbook). This sort of teacher undoubtedly gets good results with those who can survive his regime, but even then he himself feels that it is only by applying the external sanctions of examinations that students will work.

In the rod-making class, on the other hand, although there is perhaps a smaller work output, it is difficult to distinguish the teacher from anyone else at first. Instead of communication being limited to students–teacher and teacher–students, there is constant flow of comment and discussion between tutor and students, and among students themselves, and a feeling that the students are being encouraged to take responsibility themselves for what and how much they are learning.

Your leadership style

Time and time again, research work has shown how critical the style of leadership is to the success or failure of any venture, including learning.

In one of the most often quoted field studies of a type initiated by Kurt Lewin and his followers in the 1930s, the behaviour of three different types of leader was observed. A group of ten-year-old boys in youths clubs were in turn placed under three different types of leadership: 'authoritarian', where the leader was stern, bossy, encouraged competitiveness, punished those who misbehaved, and made all the important decisions himself; 'laissez-faire', where he did virtually nothing – for instance, he remained withdrawn from the boys unless he was directly asked a question; and 'democratic', where the children themselves decided what they would do, and regarded the leader as someone who could effect individual solutions of problems. All three leaders set the groups various handicraft tasks. In the authoritarian groups the boys were submissive and well behaved on the surface while the leader was present, but showed signs even then of submerged aggression, often 'mishearing' instructions or 'accidentally' damaging materials. Among themselves they were competitive and mutually disparaging. When the leader left the room they tended to abandon work instantly and to run about noisily. The laissez-faire groups did almost no work whether or not the leader was present. Under democratic leadership the boys worked well together without fear of one outdoing the other. There was little tension or aggression in the atmosphere, and, unlike the boys from the authoritarian group, some of whom broke up their models at the end of the course, all the work was regarded as 'ours' and treasured accordingly. The temporary absence of the leader made no difference to the amount of work the boys did.

This study remains a classic of its kind, especially as it shows that the same boys behaved differently with each leader. Subsequent laboratory experiments and field studies with adults have repeatedly shown that a friendly, understanding leader or teacher who encourages members to take active part in events, including taking responsibility for procedural decisions (like when to have a break, or whether or not to smoke), will greatly improve the effectiveness of the group, producing greater spontaneity, and more initiative from individual members. Dominant, aloof, authoritarian teachers tend to produce either very hostile or very subdued group members. Where actual learning is measured, the authoritarian-style group may produce more if what is being learnt is straightforward, with only one type of 'right' answer encouraged. On the other hand, where a change of attitude is involved, the 'participating' group is clearly superior.

There is some evidence, too, that creativity is more strongly encouraged in groups where the teacher does not dominate, and a good deal of evidence that the participatory group is the one most people prefer, perhaps because this is the type of group where pleasant social relationships are most likely to develop. The more people talk to one another, the more inclined they are to like one another. It is clearly much easier to retain an irrational dislike for someone you hardly ever talk to than for someone with whom you discuss and argue. Don't make the common mistake of forgetting how important these relationships are to learners because you are so preoccupied with the students' relationship with *you*.

Working in groups

Some work has also been done on the effects of deliberate competition both between different groups and between individuals. For instance, in one experiment a class of students was divided into two to discuss problems; one group was told that individual contributions made in the group would count towards their course marks, the other group was told that it was the group score which would count. In the competitive group the students were not really interested in what other people said, not friendly to one another, and produced stereotyped answers. In the co-operative group the students enjoyed themselves more, produced a greater variety of solutions, and were relaxed and friendly towards each other.

There has also been a good deal of general research into how small groups solve problems, with the idea of finding out whether it is truer to say that many hands make light work than that too many cooks spoil the broth. Common sense suggests that this will depend on what the problem is, and that it will also depend on what range of intelligence or experience is available in the group, as well as on who decides whether one solution is 'better' than another. Research here has tended to confirm that on tasks such as crossword puzzles or mathematics, which demand concentrated individual attention with only one right answer, individual solutions may be reached more quickly than group ones. But on problems, say, of politics, human relations, philosophy or the performing arts, or any subject where there might be any number of solutions, a group of people produces a far more varied and stimulating range of ideas than an individual.

Remember, too, that the co-operative group can become a powerful way of encouraging individuals to feats they could never manage on their own. Alcoholics Anonymous is one well-known example, Weight Watchers is another. In both these organizations people who by themselves have failed over a number of years to cure addictions have achieved astonishing successes with the help of a group. In teaching terms, many students who have struggled on their own with a subject can find new strength from a group, even if the skill they are learning is essentially – like solo singing, for instance – an individual activity. Perhaps it is just as Thomas à Kempis said, that 'it is the solace of the wretched to have companions in their misery', or perhaps the group really does have a dynamic effect on individual capabilities.

Summing up the differences between the extremes of tutor style, there are considerable implications for the daily business of how you conduct the course. In the student-centred group members will have discussed the aims of the course and will have themselves decided what methods are to be adopted. In the class itself there will be a constant exchange of ideas among students and a high degree of individual activity and co-operation on the part of each student, whether in discussion or creative craft tasks. Such a group will contain members at many different levels of skill and intelligence who can work together satisfactorily. The teacher's role in this sort of group will be to protect and encourage individual members, to develop a high degree of sensitivity and expertise in interpreting the feelings of the group, and to be seen by them primarily as a leader rather than as a subject expert. In many ways the teacher becomes just another member of the group. The main criterion of success in such a group is that students will feel able by the end of the course to go on learning on their own, having become capable of planning and extending their own learning.

In the tutor-centred group, on the other hand, the tutor will decide the aims of the course and will expect the students to conform to them. Those who cannot conform will tend to drop out or be made to feel uncomfortable if they stay. The tutor will do most of the talking, and if there is any discussion it will tend to be initiated by or directed at the tutor, rather than take place between student and student. The tutor will tend to see students as a remote mass rather than individuals, and will dismiss the idea that they might be hurt or discouraged by his comments, or lack of them. Such tutors will emphasize their remoteness from the group by sitting apart from them and by refusing or finding it difficult to mix with students on equal terms, or to admit to ignorance or to having made a mistake. They will encourage competition among students. There will be frequent use of tests and examinations to grade and assess students, resulting in a group where the students are streamed by ability, and where only the able students survive because the tutor finds it impossible to cope with different standards of ability in the group. Students will become completely passive and dependent on the teacher as the source of all information and are unlikely to develop much on their own.

In practice, such extremes are rare, though startling contrasts can exist, as the descriptions of the two adult institute classes quoted earlier in this chapter show.

The solution is to think of the possible range of teaching styles as a continuum which runs from 'tells the group' at one end through 'sells to' the group somewhere in the middle, to 'consults with the group' at the other end. There could be times during a course when any one of these styles is appropriate. Skilled tutors aim for a 'best fit' between these elements:

- the task;
- the time available;
- the group and its needs;
- you, the tutor, and your needs.

If, for instance, time is running out and you have to give instructions about equipment needed for the next session, then you are unlikely to have time to consult the group about their own preferences on equipment. You simply tell them what to do. On the other hand, if you are trying to change behaviours, then neither telling nor selling is likely to be effective. Learners have to make both the 'problem' and the 'solution' their own:

> I run giving-up-smoking classes at the surgery. These people are usually heavily addicted smokers who *mostly*, but not quite, want to give up. I have found over the years that it is quite pointless telling them they *must* stop, even with all my 'authority' as their doctor. They've all heard the health messages many times. The commitment to stopping has to come from them. I run the group by drawing from them individually and as a group *why* they want to stop, best ways of stopping, how to cope with lapses, etc. etc. This way I achieve roughly an 80% success rate. 'Telling' was no good – they dismissed me as a goody-goody spoil sport!

For all that, you may occasionally have to use a 'telling' style of teaching, there seems little doubt that participation and 'consulting' is a better general model. When learners contribute, they are involved and involvement of a challenging kind is one of the main routes to learning.

The group life cycle

> It was chaotic at the beginning. Rival factions from different departments, standing up making speeches denouncing the others . . . people sulking, threatening to leave – awful!
>
> I could have stood on my head at the beginning in that group for all the reaction I'd have got. I felt like coming in with a false moustache or a clown's nose to see if it would even have surprised them. Personally, I participated like mad, they never did.
>
> How can you get a good discussion going with forty large adults who sit in a room designed for twenty small children? No wonder the sessions seemed to be a bit stodgy.

Handling groups of learners can be tricky. A group has its own life and behaves in its own way and this is different from the way the individuals inside it will behave. Being prepared for some of the problems is essential if you are to be its leader.

It helps to understand that groups typically pass through a recognizable life cycle which is usually summed up as 'Forming – Storming – Norming – Performing' in that order. At the *forming* stage there is little sense of group – it is still a collection of individuals. You could say that this is typically how a course group seems at the first meeting: subdued and cautious. At the *storming* stage, people become bolder, and conflicts may emerge openly: mutterings about other people's behaviour, disagreeable arguments, jostling for dominance. This can be a difficult stage for tutors: you may have to use all your negotiating and leadership skills to prevent the destruction of your group, especially if they turn on *you*:

> I was teaching the techniques of job-searching to a group of long-term unemployed adults. This was tricky anyway because we are an area of very high unemployment. On the second day, the whole thing nearly collapsed. Mutterings about 'it's all very well for him – he's got a job' turned into openly hostile verbal attacks by one half of the group, while the other half sprang to my defence – 'give him a chance – anything's worth a try'. I calmed the whole thing down with great difficulty and suggested that we started again. The ones who were angry were given a lot of time to say what it was about me that had caused

> such attacks and the rest were given their say, too. I retrieved it by the skin of my teeth – but it was a crisis, no doubt about that.

At the *norming* stage the group has settled down. A pecking order has been established, people know each other better, they have accepted the rules and probably developed little subgroups and friendship pairs. In a short course – say, of a day's duration – all these stages can be passed through with great rapidity:

> First session – quiet and cautious. Second session – glances of irritation exchanged at 'things people say'. Coffee break. Third session – the break in the clouds . . . they've talked during coffee and have discovered that other people are not so awful after all. Fourth session – purposeful: emergence of jokes, sense of where people are going. End of day – people are exchanging addresses and phone numbers!

So at the final stage, *performing*, the group glides into action. Now they exist as a group with their own roles and rules. If you let them, they may well always sit in the same seats; they will enjoy group tasks and will carry group loyalty to great lengths. At this stage, the group has a life of its own; its power to support learning is very considerable:

> I went to a two-day assertiveness course organized by my company. It was very well run, but the best thing about it was the amazing feeling that developed very quickly in the group. The other women were so terrific – for instance, if someone who had been really shy managed a more assertive role play, there would be spontaneous applause. People spoke warmly to each other about their efforts. I've rarely seen anything so inspiring . . . it made us all achieve feats that would have been impossible alone.

A group does not reach the 'performing' stage by accident. It is the natural and positive way for groups to develop, but it happens because that is the way the tutor has nudged and pushed it. This sort of triumphant conclusion to a course is usually the result of a great deal of conscious effort and skill on the part of the tutor:

> Best of all we had an end-of-session party to which we all contributed food and drink. Very enjoyable it was too! This was an unofficial meeting in our own time, but just before the end

Mr R., who had spent most of the year making ribald jokes at my expense, presented me with an elaborately wrapped parcel containing an enormous box of chocolates and, on top, a beautifully written 'poem' dedicated to the group and listing in doggerel verse the various idiosyncrasies of the members – including one lady's habit of doing her revision in the lavatory! They insisted upon my declaiming this to them. It made a very suitable epilogue – with just the right touch of ironic banter – to what had been a very entertaining and I think mutually rewarding group.

Difficulties

Let's suppose that you are committed in principle to a participatory style in teaching. It is still possible for things to go wrong. Here are some of the common difficulties:

Talking too much

I was once myself a member of a class in seventeenth-century drama which was taken by a tutor who frequently told us that he was committed to full participation by students in the process of learning, that our learning was to be a mutually co-operative venture, and that he expected to learn as much himself from the class as we did. In fact, although a person of considerable wit and charm, he also had such an autocratic and impetuous temperament that he talked most of the time himself, answered at least half his own questions because he could not tolerate the potential embarrassment of a silence, and occasionally conducted what were indeed vigorous and searching discussions, but always with the same three or four most naturally voluble and perhaps most able students. He made a few token efforts to coax speech out of the others, but gave the impression that he probably never noticed how little they responded. By the end of a ten-week course the numbers had reduced to below half the original large enrolment, and even among the survivors there were two people who did not utter a single word in twenty hours of class contact.

One classic piece of research in the 1950s confirmed how little teachers may know objectively of their own part in lessons. Alvin Zander made a study of four teachers of adults who claimed to be committed to student participation, and found that on average they lectured for 27 per cent of the time, matched each student's contribution with one of their own, and made nine out of ten of all the procedural decisions.* Other research has tended to show how teachers may have no idea how much attention they are paying to particular students. In one study of a class of twenty-six, the teacher was found to be giving more than a quarter of his attention to the well-adjusted pupils who presumably did not need it. Even after he had realized this, he found it extremely difficult to distribute his attention more fairly.† Many teachers will recognize it as a familiar temptation to go on encouraging those who need little encouragement, and to avoid the difficult and perhaps painful or embarrassing job of helping those who may be silent, moody or unstable.

There is a simple solution to talking too much: stop. The difficulty is that the tutors who are prone to doing it are usually totally unaware that there is a problem. There is a rough and ready test for finding out if this could be your problem. Ask yourself two questions:

- Do you always follow a comment from a learner with one of your own?
- Are there people in your group who rarely if ever speak?

If the answer to both these questions is 'yes', then it will be worth taking stock of the situation – perhaps by asking a trusted colleague to observe you and your group in action.

Showing off

Here is a more subtle variant of talking too much, a hangover from the university tradition of great Oxbridge teachers who draw hundreds of students to their lectures. The number of people capable of carrying off such a feat is actually remarkably small: in the 1950s and 1960s there was the English literature guru, F. R. Leavis, in our own time there is the philosopher and mathematician, Stephen Hawking, and there is only a handful of others.

None the less, the tradition spilled over into adult education in

* Alvin Zander, 'Student motives and teaching methods in four informal adult classes', *Adult Education USA*, Vol. 2, 1951.

† J. Whithall, 'An objective measure of a teacher's classroom interactions', *Journal of Educational Research*, Vol. 47, 1956.

the earlier years of the twentieth century at a time when the working class was thought to be in need of rescue through WEA and university extra-mural education. The tradition still survives today, particularly in parts of adult education and training where students can be apparently quite happy to sit back and let the teacher get on with it. Richard Hoggart, himself an outstanding teacher of adults, has some wry words of warning which stress both the attractiveness and the dangers of this trap:

> The urge towards a generalized charismatic relationship, that way of showing off one's own personality which ends in the rhetoric of a lay preacher, is the strongest of all temptations. You have to learn to suspect those evenings when you feel a throb come into your voice, your eye seems bright and eager, and the students look up at you with a touch of wondering admiration. Two types of teacher – in any kind of education, but adult education is a specially dangerous area in these ways – should be particularly suspected: the charismatic, an imaginative pied piper of Hamelin; and the systems builder, an intellectual pied piper of Hamelin, who offers a complete guide and system to experience. Men who are a combination of both – some types of Marxist are like that – are the most dubious. Any teacher who begins to acquire fans, disciples, followers, ought to suspect himself until he has examined as honestly as he can the nature of these relationships. He may be getting between the students and their own hold on the subject. We should be glad to be judged by the degree to which our students stand on their own feet, out of our shadows. Which means we have to try to make sure they retain their freedom to be critical of us. Or, if that sounds too grand, ironic about us and towards us.*

A teacher talented in the dangerous hypnotic way Hoggart describes can easily turn his class into an audience for a personal performance. Often when students praise a teacher for being 'a good lecturer', what they mean is that he is a stimulating performer, by turns clown, tragedian, preacher, rhetorician, who rouses emotions at the time but leaves nothing for students to do themselves. Craft tutors can just suffer the same sort of temptation to show off their

* Richard Hoggart, 'The role of the teacher', in J. Rogers (ed.), *Teaching on Equal Terms*, BBC Publications, 1969.

expertise, only of course the 'performance' will take the form of a demonstration. In such cases a large part of the group will be taken up in a flawless demonstration by the teacher, which students are often quite happy to encourage.

The group is the wrong size

There are some basic laws of group life which relate to its size. The larger the group, the fewer the people who will speak. It runs roughly like this:

3–6 people:	Everyone speaks.
7–10 people:	Almost everyone speaks. Quieter people say less. One or two may not speak at all.
11–18 people:	5 or 6 people speak a lot, 3 or 4 others join in occasionally.
19–30 people:	3 or 4 people dominate.
30+ people:	Little participation is possible.

A friend who is a distinguished adult educationist, with whom I discussed this phenomenon, told me that he had once been present at an international conference of 60 people. A lecture had been given by an eminent scientist who concluded by inviting questions from the floor. 'Do you know', commented my friend, 'that the only three people who asked questions were *all* Nobel prize-winners!'

Here, then is the simple explanation for non-participating behaviour in large groups: it takes far more courage to speak in a large than a small group. Here are the comments of first, a student nurse, and second, an MBA student:

> I can talk in a group of four, I freeze in a group of ten!

> It takes guts to join in a larger group discussion: there's that awful moment when out of the corner of your eye you see every face turned to yours. You feel everyone judging you, so the temptation is to stay mum.

The ideal size for a learning group is between eight and twelve. Anything smaller than eight runs the risk that there will be too small a range of opinions and experiences. Increase the group much beyond twelve and you will inevitably find that it becomes difficult to draw everyone in.

Sometimes, however, you will find that you are landed with a larger group because administratively it is 'more convenient'. There are workable solutions to this problem.

> I plan sessions which alternate whole-group talk/discussion with lots and lots of role play in threes and fours.
>
> I give a general introduction lasting ten minutes, then I split the group into smaller groups of five or six with a problem to solve. They report back to the main group for the final 15 minutes.
>
> Pairs working on mini projects, prepared in advance by me . . .

Beware, though, of introducing small-group work without designing it carefully and thinking it through:

> My heart sinks at a conference or the like, when the session leader says brightly, 'Now we're going to split into buzz groups for five minutes' and gives you some entirely pointless 'task'. You know it's meant to encourage participation, but so often it just seems a stale and meaningless device, and sometimes, I'm sorry to say, suggests that the lecturer can't be bothered to work out something better.

The room arrangement is inappropriate

> I joined a flower-arrangement class. The trouble was that it took place in the physics lab at the local comprehensive. We sat in straight rows, so you never really got to know anyone except your next-door neighbour.
>
> The room was a great big barn: high ceilings, bare floor, hard upright chairs. The only way to get people feeling more comfortable was to set out our chairs in a circle in one corner.

Manipulating the physical shape of your group – where and how participants sit – has an enormous influence on how they behave. The key factors for maximum group contact and participation are:

- keep the space between chairs to a minimum;
- remove redundant chairs;
- establish open 'eyelines' – let everyone be able to see everyone else without having to twist or turn;
- comfortable but businesslike chairs;

- a room that just fits the group, not too big and not too small (but too small is better than too big);
- tables or desks that fit the purpose;
- thinking carefully about where you seat yourself.

There are hundreds of ways in everyday life in which the way we arrange and use the furniture in a situation is a symbolic way of showing how we feel in it, or of showing what the power and communication situation is. One chair round a dining table might have arms, it is a 'carver', and in many families this chair will always be taken by the most authoritative person and will be put at what becomes the head of the table. In most churches the parson's distinctive and influential role is stressed by the fact that he stands some distance apart from his congregation, who usually sit facing him in strict rows and are not expected to make any but a unanimous response. Quakers, on the other hand, who have no priest and who encourage contributions from anyone at a meeting, arrange their chairs in a hollow square with no special places. In an office one can expect the manager who leaves the desk to come and sit companionably beside a visitor to be friendlier than the manager who remains firmly behind it.

Exactly the same sort of symbolic representations are at work in classrooms. A class listening to a lecture will sit in straight rows facing a lecturer, who sits or stands apart. The arrangement of the chair emphasizes that the lecturer is a special person.

In a class where a little more discussion is expected, the tutor may still stand apart, but will face students sitting in two curved rows. In a craft class where the students are working individually and expect individual attention from the tutor, they will sit at tables dotted all over the room. Where they expect to help each other and work in small groups, several desks will be pushed together. In a discussion group where the tutor is no more than chairperson, the chairs might be arranged in a completely closed circle in which the tutor takes his or her place just like anyone else.

Desks and chairs themselves serve to emphasize roles and relationships. It is quite usual in most classrooms to find that the tutor's desk is larger and the chair more comfortable than the rest of the furniture in the room. It may be even perched on a platform – literally in a 'high up' place.

Tutors who abandon their chairs to stand in front of the desk or perch on it, may be able to talk more informally with students. When they are behind desks they emphasize their teacher role. In a circular or hollow-square seating arrangement, tutors who want to emphasize that they are just another member will take care to leave the special chair alone. When they resume the role of leader they will return to it.

You are sure to find that a group tries to emphasize your role as leader by creating physical space between you and them:

> I always arrived first to set out exactly the right number of chairs in a neat circle. By the time we began, I nearly always found that, mysteriously, a space had appeared between my chair and my neighbours!

> I've noticed that people will go to considerable lengths to avoid sitting next to me. In one large group I teach, students will even form a second row rather than take the last 'free' spaces at either side of me.

It's up to you how you deal with this phenomenon. Let it pass unremarked if you feel it is of no significance, or even that it is a valuable way of emphasizing your leadership role. Insist on closing the gap if 'total equality' is your aim.

Comfortable and uncomfortable chairs, large and small groups have other inescapable influences. Infant-sized chairs, apart from being extremely uncomfortable, may suggest a childish role to a student. Hard, upright chairs may communicate an unpleasantly spartan and disciplined atmosphere. One of the most difficult groups I have ever had in adult education was in an open prison where I had been asked to bring my own class to form a discussion group with some pre-release prisoners. To add to our considerable nervous uncertainty of how to conduct ourselves in so unfamiliar a setting we had our first few meetings at one end of an enormous cold hut, sitting in a circle on hard wooden chairs, and generally gazing at our knees. Discussion was slow. The improvement when we moved to a small sitting-room with easy chairs was amazing. No doubt this was partly because we had by then been meeting for three weeks but the easy chairs in themselves seemed to suggest that we could all relax, and the social rather than educational associations were a positive advantage.

It does not need elaborate research (though there has been some) to show how influential the seating is on the kinds of communication people make and feel able to make. Clearly, sheer physical distance is important. Someone sitting at the back of a number of rows is less likely to speak to the lecturer than someone at the front. For people sitting at the front, the difficulties of twisting round to address other people or even to see and hear other people will generally mean that most people listen to and encourage talk from the one person who has a good view of everybody – the lecturer. In the opposite type of group, by sitting close to people and facing them, it is extremely hard not to talk to them, which is why contributions to conversation in a circle are usually divided pretty evenly between members. After only a short time the pattern becomes well known to all the members and very hard to break. The longer a lecture pattern continues, the harder it is for the shyest, most silent member to speak; the longer the garrulous 'circle' group continues, the harder it is for them to listen to a lecture. In other words, the shape of the setting first influences and then reinforces the typical way in which the class behaves.

You should feel free to manipulate the teaching space in anyway you like, altering it frequently if necessary during each group meeting.

The institution is unsympathetic

Sometimes tutors will use the supposed wishes of the students or the supposed traditions of the institution as an excuse for dominating the class. The argument then goes something like, 'Of course the students are too dim (or too shy, or too noisy) to take much real part in things', or 'They want you to be in charge', or, more subtly, 'Of course we'd like to run things on a participatory basis but the principal prefers the traditional approach'.

Some of these alibis may contain elements of truth. Institutions, or even those outside them, may exert direct or indirect pressure on tutors. For instance, it would not be unusual in a college of further education running day-release courses for a particular firm for someone from the firm to telephone the principal to say that he thoroughly disapproved of all this discussion and poetry that his lads were getting up to on Wednesday afternoons, that they were being sent to the college to learn engineering, and if they did English then it ought to be engineering English. Pressures may not be so direct in adult education or training but they are there, and frequently exerted in gentler ways: 'I'm afraid the noise from your discussion group upset my class', or 'The local newspaper has got hold of your class social survey. They say people are complaining about answering intimate questions. Perhaps you'd better get them to stop for this week', and so on. If you think you may encounter problems of this kind, then you need to prepare the ground carefully by discussing all the issues in advance with the likely resistors.

The best way to counter opposition is to anticipate it by involving the influential people in a 'training-needs analysis'. That way they help analyse the problem *and* feel part of the solution – which can include any adventurous methods you wish to use.

The students resist

I once sat in on an industrial relations course with a group of eighteen men who were using an elegant room well equipped for small-group work, with special tables and close carpeting to deaden noise. The small-group discussion came at the end of a tiring day's work which consisted mostly of listening to lectures, with half an hour for discussion afterwards. It was clear that in their three small groups they were feeling disgruntled and had felt that they were groping for direction, even though they dutifully exchanged experiences and all spoke a great deal. After several weeks of going along with the teacher they asked for whole-group discussion, as they said they felt they could benefit more from the exchange of views among the whole group than they could in groups in six. Perhaps this was a more ambiguous situation than it at first appeared: the teacher was taking no part at all in the small-group work, but spent this part of the class 'marking the register' (having a rest). Neither was there any reporting-back session. The afternoon ended when the small groups broke up. The students made their dissatisfaction clear. The tutor didn't seem to care, so why should they? Maybe their attempts to resume whole-group work, which involved the tutor becoming group leader again, was simply an attempt to force him to do what they thought was his job.

If your group pleads for 'lectures' then clearly you must take the request seriously as a sign that something is wrong with the structure, method or content of the course. Don't leap into delivery of a lecture without a careful analysis of where the problem lies. Listen attentively to what the group has to say, bracing yourself for critical comments. The most appropriate solution will depend on the cause of the problem:

> My group didn't like 'participation'. The underlying reason was that they all lacked confidence. I had pitched the opening level of the course too high. By stepping back three stages, we solved the problem and they began to join in.
>
> Real cause – no experience of discussion. Had to have lots of patience, lots of silence, lots of coaxing . . . then it worked.
>
> . . . lack of proper motivation . . . people being sent on training courses because no-one knew what else to do with them. A fortnight away from base at a nice country house was regarded as a good chance for a rest – sitting back and 'listening to lectures'. The only way to change that was to alter the recruitment policy by insisting that the delegates were purposefully chosen, well-briefed, and turned up knowing exactly what was expected of them.

What makes a good tutor?

Many of the problems cropping up in groups come down in the end to the personality and skills of the tutor. Thinking back to my own schooldays and to the teaching I have encountered since, the outstanding teachers all shared an enthusiastic, open, relaxed style while teaching. Away from the classroom they were people of very different personality. Educational research has confirmed what most of us already know from this kind of personal experience, that effective tutors have these characteristics:

- a warm personality – ability to show approval and acceptance of students;
- social skill – ability to weld the group together and control it without dominating it;
- an 'indirect' manner of teaching which generates and uses learners' ideas;
- organizing ability so that resources are booked, administration is smoothly handled;
- skill in spotting and resolving learner problems;

- enthusiasm – for instance, an animated demeanour, plenty of eye contact, varied voice inflexion.

  She just plunged into the work of teaching us . . . inexhaustible energy on our behalf. Knew our problems before we'd seen them coming ourselves and helped us find the solution that was right for us . . . cared passionately about our progress. Loved her subject and was extremely knowledgeable in it, yet gave us all the feeling that we were experts in it too because all our efforts were bent towards our *finding out for ourselves.* Magically we always had everything to hand – books, tapes, reference material. Her husband once told me that she came home every single day utterly exhausted and threw herself on the sofa unable to speak for half an hour. I must say I wasn't surprised – we had drained her dry!

This is the sort of person who makes a naturally good teacher, but it is a style which cannot be faked. Some sage and experienced adult educationists will say that they believe in behaving as if one is transparent with a class, because one is always more transparent than one realizes. These are wise words for any teacher, but they are particularly appropriate for those who teach adults.

Checklist on understanding your group

Are you clear about whether your own 'leadership style' is 'laissez-faire', 'authoritarian' or 'democratic'? ☐

Does it need modifying? ☐

Is it easy for people in your group to get to know and trust *one another* as well as knowing and trusting you? ☐

Are you alert to the probable life cycle in your group: forming – storming – norming – performing? ☐

Do you have plans to avoid the trap of talking too much yourself? ☐

Is it normal for everyone in your group to speak in each session? ☐

Is the group the optimum size for its task? ☐

If it is too large or too small do you have strategies at hand for overcoming the potential problems? ☐

Is the room the right

- size? ☐
- shape? ☐
- temperature? ☐

Are the chairs

- suitable? ☐
- specially arranged to suit your purpose? ☐

Have you thought carefully about where to place yourself? ☐

Have you discussed any predicted special needs of your group with key opinion formers in your institution? ☐

Have you discussed your proposed teaching methods with the group? ☐

6

Teaching mixed ability groups

All groups of learners are of mixed ability to some extent. Even members of an apparently homogeneous group will still actually vary a good deal in their individual talents and interests. Nevertheless, for teachers of adults, there are often startling and obvious variations in ability, age and previous educational experience. These can pose apparently intractable problems:

> At least in school you can be sure of one thing – the children in each class are all the same age, and in our school they come from virtually identical social backgrounds since we are a neighbourhood school on a large pre-war housing estate. It amazed me to see the very same classrooms at night when I took my first adult class. It was the only 'Beginner's Woodwork' for some miles, so people drove considerable distances to attend. I expected my class to be all men, but of course there were women as well – that was the first shock. Second surprise, some of the class were clearly very well educated and had plenty of money, some were a bit down at heel, the eldest was in her seventies, and the youngest was a kid of eighteen I'd known when he was at the school as a pupil. I'd prepared a lesson on a simple joint, but I could see by the end of the two hours that I'd somehow got it all wrong. Several had never even seen a chisel before, or didn't know how to measure, while there were three or four who were expecting to get on with making big projects – a rocking chair in one case and a bed in another, and seemed to know a lot of the basics already. One of the main difficulties was having men and women in the same class. All the men had at least done some woodwork before, but not one of the women had. I worried about it for weeks, but in the end the problem solved itself. All

> but one of the women stopped coming, and I was left with a core of twelve reasonably adept regulars. I can't say I felt happy about it, but what could I have done?

The situation looks even less satisfactory when seen from the student's view:

> When it was clear that my marriage was on the rocks, I decided that I had to update my skills, so I went on a word-processing course run by a private company in the town. I was just about able to type with two fingers, but I'd never had any proper typing training. The brochure said this didn't matter. Unfortunately it did. There were 11 other people on the course. Some of them were very fast, skilled typists whose companies had sent them for updating – I don't know why, as quite a few seemed to have used a wordprocessor before. One was a freelance journalist who'd just bought an Amstrad and couldn't work out how to use it, then there were two or three people like me. The tutor's method was to give a lot of instructions all at once at the beginning of each section, then to set us all the same exercise. It was hopeless. The experienced people rattled away. Because they could type accurately they made fewer mistakes (so they didn't have to use the 'Delete' key much!) and finished first. She timed the exercises by these fast people and just said 'oh never mind, just do what you can' to the rest of us. It was utterly baffling and very discouraging: I felt very stupid. Since I was paying, I stuck it out, but it was a waste of money. Several of the other people thought the same. I noticed that the company closed down a few months later, so perhaps the word spread that they weren't much good.

Giving in to the deadly attraction of gearing everything to the needs of the most able learners was only one of the traps this tutor dug for herself. The other traps included a failure to recognize that a class of a very mixed ability means a need for a completely different approach. This tutor at least kept her class with her to the end, perhaps because they were desperate to learn and had all parted with good money. They clung to the hope that there might be an improvement, in spite of evidence to the contrary. Where classes are cheap, or the students' need is not so great, it is often simpler (as it was with the woodwork class) for the students simply to melt away:

> As tutor-in-charge I became very worried about the Social Anthropology group. It started with forty-five enrolments, and was down to eight by Christmas. I looked first at the enrolment cards and saw immediately what a problem [the tutor] had – graduates, two PhDs, lots of 'ordinary' housewives, several under-twenties with no O levels . . . I visited the class as preliminary to closing it down. It was clear that he'd made it all much much worse through his own inexperience. He didn't know anybody's name (and they didn't seem to know his). He muttered into lecture notes he seemed to be *reading* all the time. Participation was nil. Even so the surviving students appeared to be getting something out of it and begged us to let the class continue. We refused but I made sure the tutor attended our next training day.

The problems, then, are the ones I have already touched on in previous chapters. Unless the class is for some reason an unusually specialized one, it may contain students of mixed ability. Their ages may range over the whole adult spectrum. They will bring with them an astonishing variety of experience and confidence. Their reasons for coming to the class will vary, and so will their expectations. Some may be very clever, some will seem moderately able, some may have little apparent ability.

Like any difficulty in teaching there are no instant, pat solutions. However, there are several possible approaches which can help.

Administration

Some tutors are too new to teaching to realize that they are being asked to deal with an impossibly difficult group. Some of the problems of mixed ability teaching are in fact caused by inept administration. No teacher should be left unsupported to face a group 45 strong, like the Social Anthropology teacher described earlier whose supervisor eventually came to his rescue, but far too late.

It is true that sometimes an organizer must knowingly run the risk of offering a general class when the subject itself demands something more specialized. However, one way of coping with mixed ability groups is to take preventive action beforehand by making it perfectly clear to students what is on offer, first in the prospectus and then at enrolment.

The prospectus

Let's take a word-processing class as an example and imagine how the failed class described earlier might be publicized. Here are two possible advertisements:

> *Word processing for beginners.* One-week course starts Monday 15 April 9.30. Everyone welcome. Public Rooms, Smallgate. Tel ____.

> *Word processing:* one-week course, Public Rooms, Smallgate. This is a one-week intensive course for competent typists (60–80 wpm) who wish to learn the basics of wordprocessing. Some previous experience of using an electronic typewriter will be helpful. Our course is mostly based on IBM machines, using Displaywrite 4. The course will be especially useful for companies using this program, but basic principles of word processing will be taught, and students will also have opportunities to use Apple Macintosh and Amstrad WPs. Students will finish the course able to store and retrieve information on the computer, and lay out all the common office documents including spreadsheets. The course costs £000.00 per person. Tutor Mrs ____. Telephone ____.

The first entry tells a prospective student little. It gives no indication of the previous experience expected and no hint of the pace, style and final accomplishments of its graduates. It is the type of description written by people who want to hedge their bets: they are afraid enrolments will go down if they are too specific.

The second entry is a good deal more helpful. It identifies the entry level expected, is specific about objectives and makes it clear that there will be a brisk and business-like pace to the proceedings. This realistic approach will certainly discourage the people for whom the course is not intended, but then if they did enrol they would quickly find out for themselves that the course was unsuitable. 'Enrolment at any price' in practice means enrolment at the cost of student achievement and satisfaction and a high price also paid in tutor frustration.

Enrolment

There are still plenty of adult education centres which cram a year's enrolment into a couple of painful days in September – painful, that is, for the potential students and for the organizers, with scandalously long queues whose members must wait fretfully for classes they may or may not find have vacancies. Such centres are unlikely to give tutors the opportunity to see students in advance of the first class – an opportunity which, like a well-written prospectus entry, can make it much easier either to cope with a mixed ability group or to prevent its worst potential manifestations developing at all.

The best way to do this is for you to be present during the whole enrolment period, to meet prospective students, and to discuss the course with them. This way, a student who is clearly over- or under-qualified for a particular group may be pointed in the direction of a more suitable class. If you cannot be present all the time you should at least have given full and unambiguous information on the course to whomever will be enrolling students on your behalf.

Whatever your organization, it is always a good idea to ask learners to fill in a card or form asking them for relevant background information and what they hope to achieve from the course. A friendly photocopied letter from you is also helpful. This should welcome them to the course and should tell them about

- the curriculum;
- your teaching methods;
- any equipment they need to bring along;
- any work they need to do in advance of the first class.

Sensitive enrolment practices and a well-written prospectus do help head off some of the problems of mixed-ability classes. First, they help learners to match themselves to what is on offer, thus preventing the pained feelings of misunderstanding which can otherwise creep in. Most of us are actually rather good at self-selection, as long as we are given enough information to form a judgement. Second, these tactics will help you because you will then have details on your learners.

However, in spite of all this care, you may still find yourself in difficulties. A well-attested story tells how a visitor to one class was baffled by the large cards he noticed propped on every student's table. Each card had a different label. One said 7.15, another 7.35, another 7.50, and so on. When he inquired what the cards signified, he was told, 'Oh, that's when Mrs ____ comes round to give us our individual teaching!' History does not relate what the class was supposed to do during the rest of the time it met. In other words this tutor had assumed that the only way her students could learn was by demonstration by herself on a one-to-one basis. Although few tutors would evolve such an extraordinary solution to their problem, very many behave as if they believe it to be true that students can only learn when a teacher is overtly 'teaching', either by concentrating on one-to-one relationships, or by addressing the group as a whole. There will, of course, always be some occasions when one or other of these methods is the most appropriate, but there can be little justification for using either one of them all the time.

In a two-hour session with twenty students, allowing a few minutes for a coffee break and a few more for setting up equipment, if each student were to receive an equal amount of time this would only come to about four and a half minutes each. The bold students store up their queries, the shy ones say little. For most students, their exclusive time with the teacher is too short for more than a cursory inspection and general encouragement; jealous suspicions of 'favouritism' develop, and students also become far too dependent on the tutor when the aim of the tutor ought to be to encourage them towards independence.

Classroom solutions

It *is* possible to teach mixed ability groups successfully. Here is one teacher who met the challenge:

> I started my method several years ago when I had a dressmaking class where complete beginners and advanced students were all mixed up together. It was impossible to find one topic to suit everybody. I felt I wanted to give most time to the beginners, but there was also a need to persuade the advanced people to be more adventurous.
>
> I began by preparing handwritten photocopied sheets of instructions and drawings to go with sets of small pieces of fabric already cut out from my own scrap box. I seem to remember that this first exercise was a quite difficult one on pin tucking and seaming, a topic several students had been enquiring about but had been too timid to attempt. I suggested that each week we might spend half an hour on a similar project, then the rest of the time they could continue their own work. I explained that everything they needed to know to produce perfect work was

contained on the sheet and that they had no need of me for explanations except in emergencies.

There were some long faces at first but the method seemed to succeed more or less straightaway. Since each member of the group had a different fabric they naturally achieved different effects which caused a lot of useful discussion in which the students learned from each other. (I make a point of encouraging informal discussion. I always join them for this as I feel it is here that the class is really learning.)

More and more time was taken up on the 'experimental' work. It eventually spread out over the next year to designing their own clothes. The confidence given by learning on their own to master some of the most intricate techniques in dressmaking spread to the clothes they made for themselves and their children, which were creditably adventurous in design and execution.

The beginners began to feel left out so I was soon using the method with everybody. The duplicated sheets needed alteration – some proved too detailed, others too scanty – and were also too flimsy for constant use. The next lot were nicely typed and mounted on plastic card. At one stage I was nearly put back in the old situation. So much excitement, so many queries came that I almost could not cope. I started filling the work sheets in expanding document cases, compiling loose-leaf folders of reference material, card indexes and later on colour slides to which the class themselves constantly contributed and referred and to which they were directed by each week's work cards. Advanced students helped prepare material for beginners and one gradually builds up a stock of first-class material.

This was a radical solution. The reason it worked so well was that the tutor shifted the emphasis from herself as the fount of all information to a set of alternative resources. Although these were designed and indeed controlled by her, the students were not dependent on her verbally-given expertise during class time. Careful preparation meant that she could cope comfortably with both beginners and experienced learners in the same group.

If this idea sounds familiar, of course it is. It has been perfected in the UK over thirty years by the best primary school teachers. The end of the old 'eleven plus' freed primary schools from the need to stream and label children in order to get the ablest 20 per cent through the narrow gates of the exam. This freedom meant developing methods such as projects, group work and resource-based learning in classes where the most able could learn side by side with the least able without any loss of motivation in either. The outward symbol of this shift has been the change in the way children sit. In the old-style primary school, children sat in rows because they all needed a clear view of the teacher. Today, they sit round tables in groups of four or five. Because examinations dominate the secondary curriculum, the old format still holds, and the chairs once more all face the same way. This is one of the many unpleasant shocks that children experience when they make the primary–secondary transfer.

Successful teaching of adult mixed ability groups almost always involves applying the same techniques that work so well with young children: breaking away from one-pace, one-resource teaching, and moving towards flexibly-paced, multi-resourced learning.

I would not wish to claim that this is simple to carry off successfully. It takes more preparation, more organizational skill and probably more flair than traditional teaching. It has often been said about primary-school methods that a 'weak' teacher's deficiencies were more easily hidden under a talk-and-chalk method and rigid discipline whereas they are mercilessly exposed with 'modern' approaches.

However, a mixed ability group leaves you with little option but to plump for a flexible, resource-based approach, assuming, that is, that you want all your students to learn from the course.

The solution to the teaching problems of the word-processing course would be to apply these same techniques: for instance, to put all the instructions and exercises onto disk for use on each machine, backed up by a simple manual, and to encourage the learners to work through these disks at their own pace. The tutor then becomes a resource for problem-solving and explanation to anyone in difficulties. This would be much more likely to allow people of very mixed ability to work happily together.

Objectives

> I just have an idea in my head of where I want to get to by the end of the course . . . no, I never write it down.
> *Catering tutor*

> My aim is to turn them into critical, sensitive readers.
> *Literature tutor*

> I've been teaching this course for so long now that I know roughly what I think my group should be doing at any one time.
> *Bricklaying teacher*

These vague and hopeful statements could well have described my own actual practice in my early days as a teacher, though of course I would have been as capable as anyone of writing down fine-sounding words had one of Her Majesty's Inspectors happened to call.

Today I am a reformed character. I would not dream of planning a piece of teaching or training without first making a proper list of objectives. The reasons are that making such a list helps me plan the syllabus, choose appropriate teaching methods, and usefully reminds me of how little it is actually possible to achieve in the limited time available to me for the course. It also helps me to define who the course is *for*, thus again anticipating and perhaps deflecting any problems of gross extremes in the abilities of my students.

It is useful to distinguish between 'aims' and 'objectives'. 'Aims' tends to describe the pious hopes that some teachers have of their learners, or that principals often claim for their institutions:

> Our aim is to produce the leaders of tomorrow.

> We aim to produce young adults who can reach their full potential intellectually, socially and physically.

Objectives are much more precise because they list the intended *outcomes* of the learning by stating what a student who completes the course should be able to do.

I find it useful to plan objectives by taking a step-by-step approach, consisting of formulating answers to a number of questions. The first of these is: 'Who are the students?' I write an identikit portrait for myself, trying to answer these questions:

- What sort of people are they?
- What do they *want* to achieve from the course?
- What do they *need* to learn from it?
- What might stand in their way?
- What previous knowledge do they have of the subject?
- Why are they coming?

For instance, I am currently mulling over an idea for a course on running meetings.

The answers to my own questions in this case, run something like this:

> *Typical student for course on 'running meetings'*
> Age about 30, woman, senior secretary or junior researcher. Wants more confidence to speak up at internal and external meetings; for the future, needs to know how to chair, write agendas and notes. Standing in the way currently: lack of assertiveness, lack of practice in leadership. Plenty of previous knowledge of attending meetings, very little of running them. Wants this training because she can see it is necessary for career advancement.

Writing this analysis helps me be clear in my own mind about who the course is for. When I circulate a note about it through the organization, I can make it clear that the course is for beginners or near-beginners. If bogus beginners come forward (this is people who I discover or know have quite a lot of experience already) I have various options: to discourage them or arrange a more suitable piece of training; to find out what lies underneath this apparent miscasting; to accept them and use them as deliberate sources of advice and experience during the course. The point is that I can make the choice: there might be something to be said for any of these tactics. If I end up with a mixed ability class, then it is because I have weighed up the advantages and disadvantages myself: I am not helplessly accepting someone else's judgement.

Second, what do I want them to be able to do by the time they have completed the course? The key word here is 'do'. The ideal objective is one where the learner could *demonstrate competence to somebody else*, so words like 'understand' or 'appreciate' do not make for useful objectives because no two people could ever agree on what constituted 'understanding' or 'appreciation'. For instance, 'understanding the role of computers in society' could mean anything from being able to name a single multinational computer company to being able to design an acceptable IT system for that same company. 'Appreciate the music of Beethoven' might mean anything from quite liking the final movement of the Ninth Symphony to being able to make fine judgements between the performances of two great orchestras playing that symphony.

It is better to stick to objectives where the learner's achievements by the end of the course begin with words like

make	identify
plan	compare
list	solve
produce	write

For my course on running meetings, my objectives given to the students will probably look something like this:

By the end of the two-day course you should be able to:

- write an agenda for a two-hour meeting;
- prepare briefing notes for participants, if necessary;
- chair a meeting of up to 7 people;
- write and circulate notes on the meeting.

Third, by what standard would I judge whether students had reached the objective? Here, again, it helps to be specific. In the jargon, it is necessary to add 'performance criteria'. Suppose the aim is to teach someone to deflea her cat. The objective could be stated as: 'By the time X has completed this piece of learning, she should be able to deflea her cat successfully.' Ah, yes, but what constitutes 'success'? Is it a success if the cat stops scratching for a day? Is it successful if you can't see any fleas with the naked eye?

The objective will be even more helpful if it runs like this:

> By the time X has completed this piece of learning, she should be able to deflea her cat so that when the cat is combed with a fine metal comb five days later, no live fleas or larvae are seen on the comb.

The virtue of this much more long-winded version is that it would be perfectly possible for X to prove that she could indeed deflea a cat competently. Furthermore, the same criteria could be widely applied and judged.

If I apply this same rule to my objectives for the 'running meetings' course, then I also need to add 'performance criteria'. For instance to my objective on 'writing notes', I could add: 'write and circulate notes of the meeting *which are accepted by participants as a succinct but accurate record'*.

Ideally, objectives also need to state in what circumstances the objective is being applied. For instance, for my learners, it would not be fair to expect them to chair a large and tricky negotiating meeting involving outsiders, so my objectives should probably also contain a conditional phrase such as 'Given an intra-departmental meeting of not more than 10 people, could write and circulate notes which are accepted by participants as a succinct but accurate record'.

Summing up, then, a good objective will state:

- what the learner can *do*;
- under what *conditions* the learner will perform;
- to what *standard*.

Finally, who else needs to be consulted? Once you have an outline list of objectives, it is always a good idea to seek opinions on them. If you are working in industry, then ask the relevant employers or line managers. Are these the skills they want their trainees to have? Ask the learners too – is this what they think they want and need? Ask people who have done the same kind of course in the past. Most objectives have to be modified at least a little in the light of this exercise.

Writing objectives takes time and care, but it is effort well spent. It forces you to focus on what it is actually possible for people to learn in the time available, and will help you decide where you should put the boundaries on previous experience or ability in your learners. It will also help you choose the most appropriate teaching methods. If one of my objectives is that people should be able to chair a meeting, then clearly I must spend large chunks of the course giving everyone practice at doing just that, which immediately suggests a heavy emphasis on role play.

Teaching a mixed ability group can be a blessing or a misfortune. Which it turns out to be is, to a large extent, in your own hands. If the needs of your subject and the standard to which it must be taught dictate homogeneity, then you (or your administrators) need to be both honest and ruthless at the recruitment stage. If this is neither possible nor desirable, then the best solutions will lie in the direction of the kinds of resource-based learning which are the subjects of several subsequent chapters in this book. In general, the more participatory the method, the easier it is for people of all abilities to learn from the same experience:

> The previous Minister had been a rather intense academic theologian, and 'Bible study' had dwindled under his leadership to a tiny cohort of people who could keep up with his high-level dissertations. When he left, the new Minister was much more interested in lay participation and a system of 'house groups' grew and flourished. The extraordinary thing about this is how mixed they are: all ages, all abilities, yet even the more timid and really quite unacademic people have taken part and have even led the discussions. This is because the whole thing is based on *everyone* taking part. I have been at evenings where a PhD in theology has clearly got as much out of it as a new young member from the local housing estate. That's because the leadership training has been very thorough, and because we have relied on excellent videos and discussion papers and because the emphasis has been on being able to join in discussion at any level of experience or knowledge.

Checklist on teaching mixed ability groups

Does the prospectus make clear:

- the course objectives? ☐
- the teaching methods? ☐
- prerequisite knowledge? ☐

Does your enrolment procedure allow you to:

- meet students in advance? ☐
- see their entry forms? ☐
- divert them to other classes if necessary? ☐

Do you always write to learners telling them about:

- the curriculum? ☐
- your teaching methods? ☐
- equipment they need? ☐
- work they need to do in advance? ☐

If, in spite of this, you still have a mixed ability group, have you planned:

- to reduce dependence on talks and demonstrations? ☐
- to increase resource-based learning, individually or in groups? ☐

Have you written yourself a clear set of objectives for:

- the course? ☐
- for each session? ☐

7

The first session

The first session is the single most important occasion of the course. You may be feeling apprehensive – justifiably, because if you don't get it right it will be hard to rebuild the relationships. The students may feel nervous, but it is you, not they, on trial:

> The first night of the pottery class we didn't do anything at all, we just sat there while he gave us the whole history of clay. This wasn't what I'd wanted at all. Once I'd set eyes on the clay, I wanted to get going. He just talked and talked and talked. When it came to 'question time' we were all so exhausted we couldn't think of anything to ask.

> I was asked to attend a day-release course at the local tech. I wasn't too keen because it's thirty years since I was last in a classroom and I had a feeling the whole place was going to be crawling with clever dicks. I didn't think much of it from what I'd heard because we send a lot of our lads there and all they seem to do is a lot of stuff on literature and sex, watching films all day. First we had this lecture from the Principal welcoming us to the college, explaining why we couldn't use the canteen, etc., then the first lesson was a long lecture on communications. It was all way above my head and I stopped listening after a bit. I knew a few other blokes there, and one of them asked a question at the end, so I suppose he'd understood all right. The chairs were very uncomfortable and I was itching to get up and stretch my legs. Then in the last few minutes the teacher said he wanted some volunteers to give a ten-minute talk to the rest of the class the next week. It was just like the army, no one moved, so then he suddenly turned on me and said 'Will you do that? Right, ten minutes next week.' I couldn't have done it to save

my life. When I got back to the works I made an excuse to leave the course and that was that.

Such gauche and cheerless beginnings can be avoided, but it takes careful planning – some would say, cunning:

> I think of the first class meeting as a kind of first date with a desirable partner who has to be wooed and courted. Shyness is *out* on my part, while I have to recognize it as a factor on theirs. I mustn't be *too* overwhelming, but on the other hand, I have to make what is on offer seem attractive. If it isn't a success, I know they'll disappear – endless polite excuses, but I won't see them again! Since they pay on each occasion and I get a cut, it matters to my wallet as well as to my pride . . .
>
> *Aerobics teacher, Leisure Centre*

Adults are less indulgent and less long-suffering of their teachers than children. When they don't like what they find, they will stay away, even when the employer is paying.

Your plan to avoid this humiliating débâcle might fall naturally into three phases: before the class, during it, and after it.

Before the class

Find out who they are

The previous chapter has suggested how important it is to seek out as much information about your students as you can in advance, preferably by meeting them in person as well as asking them for some personal details on paper. Begin by memorizing these details before you start the course – it will be a help in getting to know the group quickly. It often matters, for instance, to find out if anyone has travel difficulties, or, if they are on a full-time training course, whether they have been able to cut themselves off satisfactorily from the demands of their normal work.

On one training scheme the mystery of why one foreman always nodded off to sleep at 5 p.m. was solved when he admitted that there was no one to take his place while he was away, so he had been getting up at 4.30 every morning to inspect the work his men had been doing the previous day.

Many adult learners find it similarly impossible to leave their responsibilities behind them and may be worrying about a new baby or a sick elderly parent or about an important project at work. Make it your business to be alert to such problems – they may explain an otherwise baffling lack of commitment to your course.

Sort out the housekeeping

A few years ago, I joined a course which met at our local concrete university. The first class was scheduled to start at 7 p.m. Unfortunately, the signposting at Reception was inscrutable, and the building itself designed to confuse, its grimy tower blocks being linked by unlabelled and ugly windswept ramps. I finally found the room after 15 minutes of searching, but alas! The venue had been changed. A notice flapped on the open door announcing a different room (one I had passed several times already in my search). The tutor gave me a hostile stare as I climbed over benches to find a seat. He was annoyed because his introductory chat was being interrupted so many times by similarly lost latecomers – indeed they kept sliding in until 7.45.

This course was not a success. Even though most people's fees were, like mine, being paid by their employers, the initial group of twenty-two was down to ten by the fourth meeting.

Most such problems are entirely preventable by careful housekeeping and good customer care:

- inform the receptionist – make sure he or she is welcoming;
- direct people with clear signposts;
- double-check the room booking;
- double-check audio-visual aids;
- arrange the room so that it suits your purpose (see pages 83–6).

Tell students in advance about objectives, syllabus equipment or reading

Sometimes students may simply turn up and enrol on the spot. But more commonly you will know who they are in advance. Write to them, introducing yourself and your course. Equally importantly, tell them what they will need to buy, borrow or do so that they come to the first class already equipped. It is frustrating all round to feel that the first time the class meets is a dress-rehearsal without props, a postponement of the enjoyable business of getting down to the real thing.

Make a plan

The first class is so important that it is always worth planning it on paper. I write myself a plan which has 'time' down the left-hand column, 'activity' in the centre and any audio-visual aids or handouts that I shall need in the right-hand column. Whatever the temptation, especially if the group is beginning to relax and unwind, I stick to my plan fairly rigidly, otherwise I find that aimless discussion can take over, and the purposeful part of the class is squeezed into a rushed half-hour at the end.

During the class

The first few minutes

The most useful comparison is to think of yourself as a host. A good host greets the guests warmly, introduces them to each other, and tries to make sure that everyone has a pleasant time. Unfortunately, it's all too easy to fall short of this ideal:

> Got to the Spanish class on time, but no teacher to be seen – she arrived five minute late, puffing and panting, but with no apology!
>
> We are sat there in silence and semi-darkness – very uncomfortable. On the dot of 10.00 the tutor walked in, switched on another light and launched straight in to a lecture on 20th-century architecture. I had no idea who the other people were. In fact the tutor never told us his name either . . .

A better tactic is to arrive in plenty of time – at least twenty minutes before the official start time. Greet people warmly at the door, ask their names, introduce them to one another.

Briefly introduce yourself to the class, telling them what your credentials are in the subject and why it interests you. Never underestimate the importance of learning and using people's names as a way of making them feel they matter to you and are part of the group. Establish whether you are going to use first names (including your own, of course) or be more formal. Either way, learn names quickly and use them often: this will help the group to do the same. Name badges can be useful but make the print large enough for people to be able to read it easily at a distance.

It sometimes helps to go round the group asking members to introduce themselves, but use this technique with caution:

> The panic which I had been feeling for some time as September approached now gripped me tight. My teaching experience had all been gained in primary schools, and although I was an English graduate, I felt very out of touch with current approaches to teaching the subject. Memories of my own schooldays supplied little that seemed relevant to adults and a search through my teacher-training course notes revealed few new ideas.
>
> I had decided to spend the first evening in getting to know the class. My method was based on one which I had previously seen used at a weekend conference where we had seated ourselves in a circle and the chairman had asked each one in turn to introduce himself to the group and explain why he had joined the course. In those circumstances the method had worked well; barriers were broken down and later we felt at ease with one another when discussing topics in small groups. But here it was not so successful. The bare-walled room, filled with adults cramped into apparently toy-sized desks, arranged with the stiff formality that is the mark of most classrooms at the start of the year, made everyone feel ill at ease. The fact that few of the group had ever tried to verbalize the reasons for their actions, certainly not before a mass of strangers, led to a series of ill-defined and repetitive statements uttered in barely audible tones and in a variety of accents, both British and overseas.

It takes confidence for students to join in on this kind of introductory round: some students may be so nervous that they fail to take in anything said by others, thus defeating the purpose. You may also run the risk of one person sabotaging your plan, as in *The Return of Hyman Kaplan* by Leo Rosten, an enjoyable book of stories about a boisterous and irrepressible character who enrols in an American night school. His teacher, Mr Parkhill, always asked his students at the first class to write on 'my life'.

> Mr Parkhill felt that nothing so promptly enlisted the interest of his novitiates, so rapidly soothed their anxieties and bolstered their morale, as the invitation to recount the story of their lives.

However, Mr Kaplan's version did not go quite as expected. When it came to his turn, Mr Kaplan's contribution was proudly written on the board as follows:

Hyman Kaplan
by
H*Y*M*A*N K*A*P*L*A*N

First, I was born.
In Kiev, in old country. (Moishe Elman, famous on fiddle is also coming from Kiev.) 'Notice the sentence structure class', said Mr Parkhill absently; his mind was not on sentence structure at all: It was wrestling with the remorseless logic of that 'First, I was born'.*

Plugging on in spite of such setbacks can still pay off, but it takes spirit:

First of all I greet them at the door. I say something, anything to them, like 'Have you parked?' or 'Found the room all right then?' Usually I've got some kind of background information from their companies on who they are and why they've been sent on the course, and I know all their names in theory – I'm just waiting to fit the faces to them.

I get them going on doing something straight away, even if it's only writing their names on a card, then I tell them a bit about myself, establishing my credentials, as it were. I know they're thinking to themselves 'He's a bit of a pusher isn't he?' but I don't care. Let them think that, I know they're still curious to know what sort of bloke they've been landed with. Then I say 'Right, now you've heard about my background – let's hear yours.' So we go round and they say 'I'm Bill Smith, I work at so-and-so's, such-and-such plant'. Usually he's so nervous he can hardly get this out without his voice wavering, so I butt in and I say 'Oh yes, Bill' (you think that's corny, but I try to get on first names straight away, none of this 'Mister' nonsense), 'you've had some trouble with the gear-cutting equipment at your place, haven't you?' He looks surprised, he's pleased, you see, and after we've had a chat about gear-cutting, he tells us a bit more about himself, and so we go on, right round the class.

* Leo Rosten, *The Return of Hyman Kaplan*, Gollancz, 1959; Penguin, 1968.

> Then I have another bit of spiel, I say 'I know when you walked up those steps, you thought "They're a funny looking lot, I'm not going to say anything." Everyone has that feeling and if you don't have it, you're so lacking in modesty, you're wasting your time here.' I go on like this for a bit – it's all to get them to relax. I go on to the real work when one or two of them start butting in and teasing each other, perhaps they cheek me a bit, or they all start grinning at one of my jokes instead of giving me the old stony stare. That's when I know we can get on with things, when they don't look at me as if I was a clockwork orange.

Depending on your subject and your students, you could also use 'icebreakers'. These are exercises deliberately designed to dismantle the barriers of shyness and reserve which most of us bring to a new group. A typical and very simple 'icebreaker' would be to seat the group in a circle and then to ask everyone to reseat themselves alphabetically starting with 'A'. To do this, of course, involves everyone asking everyone else their names. Another 'icebreaker' demands that every other person in the circle sits in a pair with the person on their right. The pair then exchange brief life histories. Now each pair joins with another pair, only this time everyone takes it in turns to introduce their partner to the other couple. Icebreakers are a form of party game and therefore fun. They are often staggeringly effective. Long-term friendships have been known to spring up under the influence of these few key minutes. However, they are not a universal cure for first-session shyness, and are probably only appropriate in groups who accept that coming to know each other quickly is part of their agenda (for instance, on some psychology or sociology courses, or at some kinds of conference).

Share and discuss your objectives for the course

If you have done your market research, then this stage need not take long because you will already have established what students think they need, and will know what your students expect to achieve. Even if you feel certain that you have got this right, and even if your students already have the course objectives on paper, it is still worth airing them. Adults are not put off by seeing the scope of a course laid out for their inspection: on the contrary, we like it.

Be prepared to discuss and to modify in the light of what the students say, or else to find convincing reasons for sticking to your original plans. There is no point in 'consultation' and 'discussion' if it is just lip-service.

Albert Mansbridge, the founder of the Workers Educational Association (WEA), tells a story which illustrates this point to unconsciously comic effect. He had been lecturing to a group of agricultural labourers about education. The audience was asked what they wanted to study. There was a long silence, then one person said 'shorthand'. Mansbridge comments:

> Such an answer might well have brought the proceedings to an untimely close, but somehow or other, perhaps owing to a hint from an understanding person, perhaps through a knowledge of the workings of the rural mind, which is not given to revealing its secrets or desires in public, I divined that they wished to study history.*

This story is recounted in apparent innocence by the man who in the same book can write, 'The initiative must lie with the students. They must say how, why, what or when they wish to study.' Of course, Mansbridge was writing at a time when adult education was the only academic lifeline for an intelligent working person, and it must have been hard for a clear-sighted inspirator to sit quiet while he saw potential talents frittered away in what to him were lowly aspirations. Cake, not bread, history, not shorthand, was what the WEA sought to bring to the working class.

Today we can be more certain that if people enrol for a class in a basic vocational skill then this is what they want.

Make a conscious effort to help students relax

You only have a short time to create the right atmosphere, and have to remember that many of your students will be nervous, suspicious, wary or just shy. This is why many outstandingly good teachers of adults seem deliberately to aim at projecting themselves larger than life and at persuading their students to do the same. Here, for instance, is an account of her aims in her first classes written for

* Albert Mansbridge, An Adventure in Working-class Education, Longman, 1920.

me in the early 1970s by a strikingly successful teacher in a North London adult education institute. She faced a number of problems: her classes were huge; her students, all foreigners, were of all ages, and at any one time they could contain as many as 16 different nationalities. At the beginning the students were shy, silent and tense. The area had many Asian immigrants and there were likely to be international stresses in the class. The students were embarrassed by how little English they knew and it had usually taken some courage to come to the class at all:

> We plunge right in on the first class meeting. My main idea is to make them laugh at me. All students can understand action jokes or facial expressions, even if they have no English, so I'm constantly acting the jokes, looking pathetic, creeping round bent up, calling myself an old lady, drawing attention to my white hair, and so on. I ask their names and perhaps if I say a few words in some of their languages – French, Spanish, Greek, Italian, Urdu – they usually understand and correct me. In this way I prove that I'm not an expert in their languages.
>
> I always make sure we do quite a bit on the first night, but it's usually very simple things like a few prepositions – under, over, on, in, out. To teach these things I get under the table, go out of the door, stand on the chair, and while there I get the class, and then individuals, to say, 'She's under the table', 'She's on the chair'.
>
> I always have plenty of real things to hand – bread, big jars of pickles (or sweets, so that we can all have one) – and we make up phrases about these: 'It's a bottle', 'It's a loaf', 'It's a sweet'. They are always things students will have seen in real life, but probably don't identify in English. At the end, I usually hold up an item and pretend I've got the wrong name – I always get a correct response. By the end of the class I make sure everyone has spoken at least once; usually I try to see that they've asked and answered a question. Quite often students who've been used to formal teaching in their own countries are very surprised at my methods. I shock some of them, I know, and they ask for books and grammar, but I concentrate on making learning enjoyable with quizzes and games. I aim to make sure everyone has a laugh during the lesson and that no one sits quietly, but that they all make great efforts to speak to me and

> to each other. I hope to send them out of my first class buzzing with excitement. After a couple of classes the students frequently bring friends, neighbours and other members of their family to join the class.

This description now perhaps has some of the dated charm of innocence – I dare say that today the same institute is as much involved in teaching 'racism awareness' as in teaching English as a foreign language. However, this tutor's inspired clowning clearly worked for her group, and would probably work for anyone who had the nerve and temperament to carry it off.

Make sure that every student achieves something

The first session must not be all jollity and nothing else; you must make sure that by the time the class ends, everyone has achieved at least one piece of relevant learning. There are various reasons why this is desirable:

- People have joined to learn. If they only wanted social contact then they would have joined a club or gone to the pub.
- It helps get them over the hump of anxiety.
- It gives a fair taste of what is to come.
- It reinforces motivation.

These first learning tasks need only be small. At the same time they should be challenging, and also carefully designed to make sure that everyone can get them right. When carried out successfully, such tactics can have powerful energizing effects.

> At the very first session we all had a go at directing a caption-change sequence to music – 'A – you're adorable . . .' etc. Looking back it seems exquisitely simple. At the time it was terrifying . . . but fun and achievable. Everyone had a go and more or less everyone went away on a 'high' – we'd sat in 'the hot seat' and got pictures on the screen!
>
> *Trainee Television director*

> In the first ten minutes of the first class, every single one of us took our feet off the bottom. OK, it was using a float, a rope or armbands, it wasn't 'real' swimming, but considering that we were all total non-swimmers it was amazing. Personally I was

> bursting with pride that I'd got over a lifetime's fear. The boost to my morale was so tremendous that I actually swam a few strokes unaided during the second lesson and swam a whole width during the third.

These first tasks must also be true to the focus of the rest of the course. Don't introduce bogus exercises which will make the students feel patronized later; keep the methods of the first session consistent with whatever you plan for later on.

> She kept telling us that the course was all about 'participation' and 'our contributions would be a valuable part of our learning'. The trouble was that the whole of the first day was taken up with lectures – there was no 'participation' to be seen anywhere.
>
> *YTS trainee*

This kind of difficulty sometimes happens because people are thought to need a dose of 'orientation' before the 'real' work of the course begins. If this tends to happen on your courses ask yourself whether it is essential for it to happen face-to-face. Might the same 'orientation' be achieved more easily and less obtrusively by giving people a paper to read, an exercise to do or a video to watch in *advance* of the first meeting?

Start and finish on time

Be wary of waiting for latecomers, however tempting it may seem. The people who have arrived on time will feel let down; soon, everyone will start coming late because 'the class never starts promptly'. If you start late but finish on time, you may look as if you are cheating your students of their due. If you 'make up for it' by finishing late, then your final few minutes are likely to be disrupted by people creeping out. Begin and end as you mean to go on: promptly.

After the class

Some assessment, however brief, is usually wise. How did it seem to go? Did everyone in the group speak? Do you now know everyone's name? If the group remained stiff and shy, what can be done to help participants relax? Don't be afraid to ask the students what they think. While very few will be prepared to offer blunt or negative criticism, even their evasions may help you plan an effective follow-up. If it went well, can put your finger on why?

If it went badly, don't immediately assume the worst. The group may simply be taking a while to shake down (see page 77 for more on this topic). Alternatively, you may have to think again. Are the objectives right? Have you chosen the most appropriate methods? Have you done enough to create a positive social atmosphere? Is your own approach dynamic enough? Were all the students involved or did some sit on the sidelines? Swift, if painful, reappraisal can often retrieve even the most difficult situation:

> We were acutely short of people to teach our first aid classes, so in the beginning there was an element of taking whoever was qualified and available. I was concerned at the poor attendance at one centre, so I went to sit in at the first session of a new course. This chap had it all wrong. He was a dedicated first-aider of many years standing but without a clue how to put it over. He started with 20 minutes of endless sermonizing about why first aid matters, while staring at the ceiling, told several people off for being 'late' (without enquiring why or waiting for apologies), barked out orders about taking the pulse, then did a demonstration of types of bandage and bandaging. Only two people dared ask questions. Most departed muttering and raising eyebrows. I took him aside afterwards. The poor chap knew all wasn't well, but didn't know how to begin putting it right. I suggested that he thought again about his basic aims: what people could *do* was surely more important than what thoughts people had in their heads? All his effort was going into trying to achieve 'Rightthink'. This was a revelation to him: together we planned a second session which was built around four tasks to be done in pairs, each one followed by discussion. He did indeed have a very small turn-out for his next class, but it went much better. From then on, he went from strength to strength. Although that particular course never regained its numbers, they didn't drop significantly after the second meeting, and his next course was 100% better.

Checklist on the first session

Are you already well informed about the background and motivation of every member of the group? ☐

Have you sent them:

- a list of objectives? ☐
- the syllabus? ☐
- details of reading/tasks/viewing/they should do in advance? ☐

Have you:

- confirmed the room booking? ☐
- briefed the receptionist? ☐
- put up signs? ☐
- booked audio-visual aids? ☐

Have you planned:

- how to arrange the room? ☐
- how to introduce yourself? ☐
- how to introduce students to each other? ☐
- whether to use first names? ☐
- how to discuss course objectives? ☐
- how to help students relax? ☐

Have you designed and prepared a challenging piece of learning that will involve every student? ☐

Have you made provision to find out what the students feel about the class? ☐

8

Lectures and demonstrations

One lecturer used to glow with excitement as he spoke. His enthusiasm was terrific and he was a most articulate speaker. He never paused at all, but he often used to say at the end, 'Well that's the first time I've ever felt I've understood that topic'. It never occurred to him to ask whether we had understood it! Usually we were lost after the first five minutes though everyone used to enjoy his performance.

The cookery class took place in an old Nissen hut, very cramped. Most of the class consisted of demonstrations by the tutor. There were eighteen of us and she used to get us crowded round her table. If you were either in front of her or in the second row you didn't have a hope of seeing. Her table was big and high, so the only students who got a good view were the two or three lucky ones who tucked themselves right behind her.

Training conferences criticize them, research proves their inadequacies, yet lecturing and demonstrating are still probably the most widely used teaching methods of all in adult education. In many cases the reason is the sheer force of tradition.

First, there can be tremendous pressure from students for a method they already know – and everyone knows the lecture method, after all, because we have all been on the receiving end of it as children. Second, nothing is asked of students other than the appearance of polite attention. This may particularly suit a group of nervous new students, apprehensive about the demands more obviously 'active' methods may make on them. In groups where attendance is compulsory, lectures and demonstrations notoriously allow students to daydream, write letters or even to gossip in whispers. Most respectably, many adult groups like a method where the teacher puts on a show of expertise because this is an assurance, at least at first, that they are being taught by someone 'really good'.

Sheer inexperience and lack of training drives many teachers to assume that talking all the time is the same as 'teaching'. For the same reason, that crucial distinction between teaching and learning has never become clear in their minds. As Postman and Weingartner remark, to say

> 'Oh, I taught them that, but they didn't learn it' . . . is on the same-level as a salesman's remarking, 'I sold it to him, but he didn't buy it'.*

Lecturing and demonstrating sometimes appeal to organizers on the grounds that they are 'economical' ways of using a teacher's time: they do not involve elaborate technician or administrative support. However, no teaching method can be described as economical if it fails to meet the prime objective of helping students learn.

Some teachers, of course, are drawn to teaching simply because they are good at talking, and enjoy it. Even teachers who are initially shy of their class may discover to their own amazement that the chance to talk uninterruptedly goes to their heads:

> It's like a drug once you've got a bit of confidence. You see the class sitting there and they're all listening to you! It's terribly flattering! You begin to think you're wonderfully eloquent and clever. It's only if and when the numbers drop off that you wonder whether you have quite the gifts of rhetoric that you hoped.

Earlier chapters have drawn attention to some of the major disadvantages of methods like lecturing and demonstrating, but it is worth reiterating them here, too. They are a strain on the already weak short-term memory capacity of adults. They proceed at one pace, which is most unlikely to suit even a majority of the class. Adults learn best through participation and activity, both of which are absent from straight lectures and demonstrations. Research has also consistently shown that lectures are a poor method of changing attitudes. In one classic experiment in the 1940s, Kurt Lewin compared the effectiveness of discussion and lectures in persuading housewives to try serving whale meat. Thirty-two per cent of the discussion group members claimed later they had actually served

* N. Postman and C. Weingartner, *Teaching as a Subversive Activity*, Penguin, 1969.

whale meat, compared with a minute 3 per cent from the group which had received a lecture.

Feedback is difficult, too. Once launched on what to you is an enjoyable exposition of your subject, it is easy for you to be blind to boredom, restlessness or incomprehension in your class. Adults are, in any case, often diffident about admitting there is a process or idea they have not understood. Conventional teaching techniques like lecturing and demonstration frequently help teacher and learner conspire together to cover up failure:

> The do-it-yourself class was taken by a retired local builder. I remember the time we 'learnt' plastering. He'd just go sweeping up the wall – 'Whoosh!' lovely. He talked all the time, but we were never told how to go 'whoosh' ourselves. However, he did pause for a few seconds from time to time to say 'Any questions?' There never were any. To answer our questions he'd have needed to go right back to minus square one and he made you feel he was going to get through his syllabus or bust, so we let him get on with it, nodding all the while as if we did understand. It was less trouble to leave the class than to explain to him that he was going about fifty times too fast.

Even the claim that lectures can be 'inspirational' may be more pious hope than reality. Most of us have sat through innumerable lectures of one sort or another, but how many are truly memorable in retrospect? Most tutors are simply incapable of routinely supplying the acting ability, originality and panache which an 'inspirational' lecture requires.

In spite of all these disadvantages, both lecturing and demonstrating have their place in the range of techniques suitable for adults. Lecturing may be a poor way of stimulating thought or changing attitudes, but research has consistently shown that it is at least as good as (though not better than) most other methods at teaching information.

Lecturing seems to be an excellent way of supplying the framework of a subject into which students can slot more learning as they acquire it through other methods. Demonstration also has advantages. It shows what a skilled performance looks like and provides a trail of visual clues which are much easier for students to remember than words alone.

However, you need to employ both methods thoughtfully. As

with every type of teaching technique, they should never be the sole methods used and you can improve their effectiveness immensely by careful preparation and presentation.

First, it is best to keep them short. Fifteen or twenty minutes of an uninterrupted 'performance' is as much as most adults can absorb. The limit for demonstrations probably ought to be even shorter – five minutes.

Second, all lectures and demonstrations should have a clearly defined beginning, middle and end: clear, that is, to the tutor and clear to the students, and it always helps a group to know what a tutor's objectives are before he begins. Here is a distinguished tutor of flower arrangement, whose crisp approach could hardly be bettered:

> I teach a lot of beginners' group even now. Because I'm fairly well-known there's lot of pressure on me to put on a great show. That's fine for big events where people really just want to be entertained, but I refuse to do it for the 'real' classes. I make them do the work. My own demonstrations I keep really short. For instance: 'I'm going to show you today how to use this foam block, because this is the simplest way of supporting an arrangement and I want you to go away from this class completely competent in its use. I'm going to show you first how to prepare it, then how to put flowers into it, then I'll go on to show you some ways of hiding it in the container. After that, I want you to practise on your pieces using the plant materials you have in front of you.' This may seem a mouthful, but it doesn't really take long to say, it prevents misunderstandings about my role and it gives them all the main points to expect. At the risk of seeming to labour it, I punctuate my demo by saying, 'Well, that's how you prepare it . . . now on to how to use it', and so on.

In other words, this tutor uses a short, intensive presentation followed immediately by opportunities for the group to practise. This way both she and the group can immediately see what the students have understood, and they reinforce their learning through practice.

This technique has innumerable possible variants. Some of these would include short lectures or demonstrations interspersed with small-group discussions, individual projects, audio-visual material like tapes, slides and questionnaires to be answered on the spot. The appropriateness of each will obviously depend on the subject and the group, but they all have the advantage that they do not strain the normal attention span of adults beyond its natural limits.

In the lecture or demonstration itself it will help considerably if you keep scrupulously to main points. The intricate examples, meandering anecdotes and funny stories which may enliven a printed page are usually simply a distraction from the meaning of a verbally delivered argument, where the audience is committed to the lecturer's pace.

Many adult students are poor at notetaking. Few of us learn at school how to take the sort of brief, well organized notes which have real meaning after the event. The process of notetaking itself can also be a diversion from understanding. An adult student who is frantically trying to cram down every word a lecturer says may have understood much less of the content than a member of the same group who has concentrated entirely on what you are saying or doing.

Nevertheless, almost all adult students need to have written reinforcement of the content of a new piece of learning. This has the dual purpose of making people feel more secure and of helping them to retain new material. Handouts are less distracting after a meeting than before; you also need to lay them out carefully. Cramped, elaborate, over-lengthy material is usually a mistake. In spite of the best intentions, few students will ever bother to read it.

Giving a lecture or a demonstration requires a special kind of self-confidence. It is alarming, especially if you are a new tutor, to feel the scrutiny of so many pairs of eyes. This alarm is often well justified. The longer you continue your solo performance, the more opportunity you are giving your group for critical appraisal of your mannerisms, dress and voice:

> It's almost like coming into a room naked. You know they can see every tremor of your hands, hear every shake in your voice, observe every change of colour, notice only too well when you're not completely master of your material. After all, what else have they got to look at!

> It was his voice that got me in the end . . . it just ground on and on. And he always had stains on his tie!

There is no doubt that lecturing exposes mannerisms ruthlessly, and most of us have little idea what our own peculiarities are in this respect. The uncompromisingly truthful image given by video can be a valuable aid to training here, though you may need to be protected from the shock of its first impact. Failing the luxury of video, observation from a frank, tactful and experienced colleague may be a good second best.

There are some common mannerisms it is worth looking out for and checking. In general it is always better to re-engage people's attention by scanning the room constantly ('the lighthouse effect') than to gaze fixedly at one neutral spot, or even worse, to address only half of a room. It is better to avoid the temptation either to pace up and down restlessly or to stand rooted unnaturally in one spot. A hesitant delivery punctuated by constant umming and erring can be wildly irritating for listeners, as can the staccato speed of a lecturer who has failed to think out timing realistically. Pausing to ask a question and then not waiting long enough for a reply will eventually drive students to permanent silence. Writing copious notes on the blackboard during a class always means that you have to turn your back on the group, with consequent loss of their attention. It is better to prepare blackboard notes before the class arrives, or better still, to use an overhead projector instead (so that you can write while still facing the group).

Many demonstrations are of little value unless they can be seen from the operator's point of view. If they are seen from the front, at the very least the student must mentally reverse all the processes. Turning the work to face the students is not the solution as it destroys the natural rhythm of the action. Large mirrors are invaluable here, but failing that, group the students behind you.

Similarly, skills teachers often do not realize how much their own skill depends on the way they choose, hold and handle equipment, because they have not analysed it in enough detail. For instance, a dressmaking student attempting to cut fabric with medium-sized scissors will be doomed to failure. Success depends on using heavy shears, large enough for the bottom shaft to contain all four fingers of the hand, and then on opening the blade wide and keeping it steady against the table. This is second nature to a good dressmaker, but far from obvious to a beginner. It is equally difficult for novices to judge their own efforts. If you are giving a demonstration, then always try to include some information on what constitutes success or failure in performance.

> I'd literally never done any embroidery before and didn't know a single stitch. She would pick up my sampler with a worried look and say sadly, 'No, no that's not right, you see it's too tight', or whatever. So often I nearly said back, 'But why ever didn't you point that out when you were showing us in the first place?' She just did the stitch – very quickly – gave us each a diagram and then left us to it. I never had much idea what the final stitch was supposed to look like.

As with every other type of teaching method, you need to arrange the room and its furniture carefully in advance. Spare chairs are best removed altogether. Curved rows will give a greater feeling of 'belonging' and therefore more chance of participation than straight ones. A hollow square round a table will encourage more questioning than rows. A large room provides bad acoustics for a quiet voice and encourages the development of vast spaces between students. Students who need to take notes need a firm surface to rest on.

In general, lectures and demonstrations are probably best used in short bursts, with frequent recourse to alternative methods of learning like discussion, individual practice, projects or reading. Far too many lecturers and demonstrators assume that their listeners have some hole in the head into which information can conveniently be poured. As Thomas Carlyle wisely said, 'Too much faith is commonly placed in oral lessons and lectures. To be poured into like a bucket is not exhilarating to any soul.'

Checklist on lectures and demonstrations

Have you planned to restrict your own talk or demonstration to no more than twenty minutes? ☐

Are you reserving lectures for occasions where a 'framework' is useful for your learners? ☐

Does your talk always have a clear

- beginning? ☐
- middle? ☐
- end? ☐

Do you always keep to simple main points? ☐

Do you follow up with

- a well-designed printed handout? ☐
- other, more participatory methods? ☐

Do you know what your own verbal or bodily mannerisms are? ☐

Have you got them under control? ☐

If you are demonstrating, are you certain that all learners will be able to see from your point of view? ☐

9

Case studies, role play, simulation and games

In a mining town in the North of England a group of twelve miners starting a four-year day-release course grope painfully after the skills of public speaking by acting out a five-minute debate based on the national conference of their own union. It is the first time many of them have ever spoken in public. They make short, stumbling, but carefully researched speeches. This is role play, bordering on simulation. At what appears to be a completely different intellectual level, a group of new training officers several hundred miles away wrestle with problems of personnel selection by basing their discussions on a folio of documents prepared by their tutor and drawing on a real-life example. This is case study. In another setting, totally different from either of the other two, a group of trainee teachers, many of them mature students, study international relations by, over several days, dividing into four groups representing four different countries, and jockeying for prestige, economic advantage and political power, with much of the seriousness and intensity that such activities must have in the real world. This is simulation, but, since each move involves points won or lost and in the final outcome one group is declared the winner, it is also an example of academic gaming.

In all these groups the tutor had found a solution through simulation and case-study techniques to the problem of how to involve adult students in the acquisition of an apparently intractable and complex mass of knowledge. The easy, neat method in every case would have been to deliver a lecture. The rules of debate, along with one or two tricks of style, could probably be explained in two hours of lecturing; similarly, the rudiments of personnel selection, or the dynamics of international relations, could no doubt have been tidily and briefly presented in lecture form. However, none of these teachers thought that it would fully meet the need of their students who, they felt, ought to experience for themselves the intricacy, excitement and perplexity of acquiring and practising skill. In other words, these tutors were not so much concerned with themselves and their own performances as with their students; they were not so much concerned with teaching as with learning.

There is nothing especially difficult or even novel about using simulations and case studies. Simulations will be familiar to anyone who has ever been involved in the army's military training exercises or to anyone who has seen primary-school children engaged in activities such as playing shop in the classroom. Role playing is frequently used in teaching and learning dramatic art; television documentaries have made us all familiar with the case-study approach, and academic games have their origins in games such as chess, monopoly or more recently, war games.

The simplest way of understanding these four techniques is to look at them as four increasingly elaborate and participatory versions of the same basic art – a way of learning general principles through being involved in a particular situation, usually one which could occur in real life, but with some of the real-life time-intervals and distracting detail smoothed out for purposes of laying bare the essentials.

Case studies can be prepared through folders of documents, collections of descriptive material, tapes, video or film, or mixture of all these, and would be presented to a group simply as the basis of discussion. Role playing takes the process a stage further, when members of the group act out and improvise roles and situations using the information they obtained from the case-study material. This might become a full-scale simulation if it were carried out continuously and intensively over several hours using fairly elaborate printed or recorded material, with fresh problems and complications introduced from time to time by the tutor. It would become an academic game if it were conducted by competing teams or individuals, who are awarded points on the basis of moves and decisions they make in relation to one another.

How is this type of classroom exercise organized and carried out? Some role playing is so simple that it hardly needs any preparation at all and is absorbed without fuss into work already being done. For instance, in a discussion on running meetings, it would be perfectly natural for a tutor to suggest that instead of simply talking about different kinds of chairmanship, the students might actually try them. In language teaching, role playing may seem a normal extension of work done practising dialogues and drills, and only becomes more recognizably something novel and different when the teacher sets up a 'scene' with the appropriate props.

For instance, in one French conversation class the tutor bases the first part of the class time on an episode from a broadcast language series where the characters are ordering food in a restaurant. The students sit in their normal places while they are repeating the dialogue and drills, but they then move in groups of four to a table in one corner of the room which is perfectly laid out for a meal. The tablecloth, wine, knives and forks, butter, mustard, menu, breadbasket and, finally, money are all French. The students 'play' the characters in the series, but extend the dialogue according to improvisations of their own and in response to the teacher, who sometimes plays waiter, sometimes another diner. After corrections and discussion they then play the same scene again.

Some tutors prefer to involve members of the group in researching the case-study material themselves: preparing speeches for a debate, or preparing a case for negotiation in an industrial agreement is one way of doing this. In this case the tutor simply presents the group with the barest outlines of the situation a week or a few days beforehand. Others favour variations on what is known in management training as an 'in-tray exercise', where the group members are presented with a batch of case-study material – letters, records, memos, press reports – such as might appear in an in-tray, and are required as individuals and under considerable time pressure to reach the kinds of decisions they may need to make in real life.

More usually, tutors will involve the whole class in group activity, either all together, in small groups, or in small groups which watch each other and then discuss. Sometimes they will deliberately hold back certain crucial pieces of information and will wait for the group to ask for it; sometimes they will supply a group or an individual with background information or documents not available to the others. Here is one such example:

Dealing with subordinates

Late without leave

Time available. One and a half hours.

Method. The group should divide into three groups of five. There will be thirty minutes for discussing the case and trying to arrive at a solution.

The groups reconvene, and each group will role play its solution to the others. The tutor will play the role of John Pickles and can be asked for further information during the pre-role-play session.

The final three-quarters of an hour will be spent in discussing the various solutions and in exploring the supervisory problems arising out of this sort of issue.

Background information: Butchards, a medium-sized engineering firm, has recently recovered from two serious disputes over pay and working conditions. The men in the 'black' machine shop had complained that their 'black money' for particularly unpleasant work was not high enough. 'Black money' was increased as a result of the strikes, but only to about half the amount asked by the union. Management have said that the order book was too slim to bear a greater increase. Since the disputes they have been making a concerted drive to reduce absenteeism and lateness. After recent negotiation with the shop stewards, all employees have received notices in their pay packets to the effect that persistent lateness without good reason will be followed by dismissal as gross misconduct. The shop stewards are uneasy about the agreement, which they do not think would stand up in law, and are looking for a test case which they hope they can also use as a lever to reopen the 'black money' negotiations. The works manager has promised that there will always be proper investigation of every case. He avows that victimization is not what management wants.

Characters and situation. Bob Painter is twenty-four, a semi-skilled fitter in the 'black' machine shop. Well known as a live-wire, enjoys practical jokes, prone to making provocative statements about workers' control in China. Bright, intelligent, can be every supervisor's *bête-noire.* Never actually puts a foot wrong, has excellent production record. His first serious mistake ever is to be a regular three-quarters of an hour late three mornings running. He offers no excuse, doesn't speak to anyone, goes straight to his work, ignoring whistles and jokes from the other men.

Harry Fletcher is thirty-three; has only just been appointed supervisor in this section, traditionally the toughest in the factory. He takes his job seriously and has been given strict instructions by management to enforce the new rule on lateness. He sees Painter arrive late, tells him he's had his last chance, and sacks him on the spot. Painter leaves without a word.

By midday John Pickles, aged forty-two, experienced senior shop steward, has brought the men out in his section. Their stoppage can halt the whole factory within twenty-four hours. He says the men will not go back to work until Painter is reinstated. His advice to Painter is to take the company to a tribunal for wrongful dismissal.

What does Fletcher do?

In this exercise the part of the shop steward was played by the tutor. He is the only one who 'knows' that Bob Painter's wife is in hospital with a threatened miscarriage and that he has been made late because he has had to get his five-year-old daughter off to school himself. He does not reveal this information unless absolutely obliged to. The roles are played successively by three different groups of students and then analysed by the whole group. Each 'scene' lasts only five minutes, but the whole exercise takes an hour and a half of class time because there is detailed discussion of company rules, of the legislative framework, of procedure for avoiding disputes in the engineering industry, of union rules, and of the human problems created by being charged with responsibility for discipline in industrial situations.

The second example is taken from a full-scale simulation designed to suit a three-hour session planned for a group of parents on 'Education Today'. The simulation centres on a case study (details disguised but taken from a real-life case) of an eleven-year-old whose parents were faced with the tricky problem of wanting their child to go to a different school from the one in which she was offered a place by the education authority. The aims of the simulation were: to inform parents about the current system in their area; to explain their legal rights within it; to explore some of the personal stresses involved in parent–school relationships; and to discuss the criteria on which choice of school might be based.

The documents themselves would be too lengthy to reproduce here but they included:

1 The child's last primary-school report.
2 A medical report.
3 Two essays written by the child on 'My Ideal School' and 'My Family'.
4 Confidential report on the child from the primary-school head to the chief education officer.
5 Copies of correspondence between parents, heads and the chief education officer.
6 Long extracts from the two secondary-school prospectuses.
7 Extracts from relevant Education Acts.
8 Extracts from 'Manual of Guidance' for parents.

Advantages

When done well, what are the advantages of this type of learning? First, the element of realism makes it an eminently suitably way for adults to learn. Adults are impatient of teaching which seems remote from the realities of whichever skill they are learning; we want to feel that no time is wasted on vague theory which is going to be of little real relevance and practical value. Thus, if a course for managers is called 'Managing Discipline' the course members may not take at all kindly to lectures on economic or historic theory, however vital the lecturer might feel this information is to understanding current conflicts. Members of such courses are inclined to say that since they conduct their real-life negotiations in an atmosphere of hustling, keen controversy, they expect to see the same atmosphere understood and catered for on the course. It is even better if the same realistic conditions can enter the process of learning itself, only in a way that more information can be fed in, in conditions of more certain control than is usual in real life, where inflamed or tender feelings can mean a stubborn refusal to accept new information at all. The realistic atmosphere in simulation is achieved through the careful preparation of the stimulus material, and also by the fact that students take roles where they start behaving as people might in a wider variety of situations than is possible in real life.

Simulation can also bring an element of realism and excitement to academic subjects by inviting decisions in a re-created historical, geographical or sociological situation. Thus students of history who might be studying the Battle of Waterloo could be given maps of the battleground, pins to represent groups of soldiers in the different armies, letters, memoranda, biographies, and so on, and could play out for themselves the crucial moves of the battle. In teaching geography to children, some successful games have been developed around events such as the building of the great North American railways, where children have in fact learnt the geography of the country, the map of the routes, and the reasons railways were built when and where they were through the use of a geography game. No doubt simulations could be developed along the same line for adults.

A second important advantage of role playing and simulation is that they are entirely active methods of learning. In earlier chapters I have tried to show how important activity is to adult learning, and have stressed how adults need to avoid being 'told' how to do something, but need instead to try it out for themselves. Indeed, simulation may offer a unique chance in certain subjects to bridge the gap between theory and practice. This can be one of the most unyielding problems of planning of a piece of teaching where, as in management or teacher training, students will frequently complain that the theory they learnt was a hopelessly inadequate preparation for facing real life. Some kind of simulation or role play may be the most effective way that managers can learn how to conduct an interview or chair a meeting. It is also an excellent way of generating a variety of solutions to problems, for instance, complex interpersonal situations where there is rarely one 'right' answer.

A further advantage of simulation and role play here is that because it is a realistic, active method, it has many of the features of learning in real life, with the powerful difference that in real life mistakes made can be expensive, disagreeable and mortifying. In role play mistakes can be made without retribution. The atmosphere of calm analysis and good-humoured support from tutor and other students makes it possible to see why mistakes have been made and to learn to avoid them in future. In this way a student, who in a business game makes a gross error which in real life would have cost her her job, can step back and analyse what moves led her (or the character she was playing) to act as she did. An added convenience is that because of its telescoped time-scale, simulation can present students with situations they are unlikely to encounter every day, and might indeed wish to avoid, but which nevertheless they ought to be prepared to meet. Thus role play and simulation in a public-speaking class might introduce a particularly odious heckler character; a management course for senior nursing officers might include a difficult situation both with clinical and surgical colleagues.

In a full-scale simulation this telescoped time-scale has the further advantage that it makes it possible to see the effect of your decisions and actions in a rapid way that is not normally possible in real life – in other words, there is almost instant feedback.

Because role playing usually arouses powerful emotions in those who take part, it can be a potent and valuable method to any tutor whose subject involves the development of sensitivity and tolerance. Crude attitude-change is not generally held to be a desirable educational aim in education, but increasing understanding in a way that may lead to attitude-change certainly is. In subjects such as politics, sociology, industrial relations, religion or literature, many issues can only be approached through a genuine understanding not just of one other point of view, but of the possibility that a whole range of viewpoints may be equally valid. Thus managers, often reluctantly persuaded at first to prepare a set of union as well as management cases for a piece of role playing, may come to understand the strengths and weaknesses, the varying opinions at different levels of seniority, of both management and union in a way that would be impossible from a more passive, intellectualized analysis. Where 'role reversal' is used (after the first run-through, the participants play each other's roles), this effect is particularly noticeable.

Another benefit of this kind of role playing and simulation is that their real value is often in the 'social skills' they teach. Supporters of this point of view would say that what is important on many courses is not so much absorbing the content of any particular mass of information as learning to understand how one's own behaviour appears to other people, to work in a group and to solve a problem, to accept other people's solutions, their contributions and their right to disagree. Where 'how' something is said is more important than 'what' is said, role play may, indeed, be the only way of learning.

Specific aims

Most people enjoy role playing and simulation. But the benefits are far from being confined to the emotional delights of acting out and creating conflict, discussion and debate. Role playing and simulation can be designed specifically to meet some of the fundamentally serious aims of any course – to teach people how to acquire, evaluate and use information. Thus, in the miners' day-release class, the second of the debating exercises was a motion on whether or not 'social wages' ought to be increased. Chairman, proposers, opposers, seconders, and speakers from the floor had all been asked to prepare their material over the fortnight between class meetings. The speeches revealed that the students had been driven for their resources to Blue Books, to books on social policy, to newspaper libraries and to their own remembered experience. This information had to be collated and assessed for what it was worth and presented cogently to the rest of the class. This was a class whose participants' preliminary education, such as it was, had been unsatisfactory, and who had barely even written a letter or read a book for perhaps fifteen years. Yet their speeches showed that the processes of active search, assessment and presentation of information had already begun. Even more so, in the burst of relieved and flowing discussion that followed the tension of formal debate it was possible to see how fact, opinion and rumour were beginning to be weighed with shrewdness and insight: 'How do you know that people come from abroad just to get our welfare benefits? There are firms in France and Germany who *give* more away than the state does here.'

On a much more elaborate scale, another group, who had enrolled for a course in urban planning, undertook a simulation which was worked in pairs over two intensive four-hour sessions separated by a week. To work out several possible solutions to a single problem in traffic control and urban redevelopment, participants were obliged to look up, absorb and use some or all of: Town and Country Planning Acts; several classic studies in urban sociology; local history; academic analyses and appreciations of Georgian architecture; and some elementary principles of civil engineering. During the course of the simulation their tutor presented them with additional complications in the form of resolutions passed by a local pressure group, or announcements of new findings on sites of historical value. Here, the group was involved in a highly sophisticated and elaborate project involving research skills, information retrieval and problem-solving, as well as learning to weigh social priorities and to argue and present a case in a final report. The students' own opinion of the exercise was, devastatingly, that they had learnt more in the two simulation classes and in the following class devoted to discussion and analysis than they had learnt in all the rest of the course put together.

Student involvement

There does not seem any doubt that simulation and role playing generate intense involvement among those taking part and that it is an excellent way of motivating people who might find it difficult to learn in other ways. It is almost impossible to remain aloof and uninvolved. Even the most stately student usually finds it hard to stay outside. Most students start by thinking it is going to be a laugh, something they will go along with to humour their tutor. They then rapidly pass to the stage where they are involved but keep some superficial sense of joking distance or irony. In a class such as the urban-planning group where the basic emphasis is on academic skills this often remains the predominant mood. Where the whole group is also involved in role playing, even this mood passes, replaced by an entirely absorbed seriousness for the task in hand.

Simulation and role playing are immensely adaptable for classes of mixed ability. They can offer natural opportunities for working in groups, for occasions where students of different abilities can help each other, and where distinctions between the bright and not so bright can at least be blurred if not extinguished altogether.

The tutor's role

Many tutors are bothered by the apparent inevitability of their own dominance in the classroom. Simulation involves a fundamental change in your role. You are still very much in the centre of things since you prepare at least the initial materials, and in the class you will usually retain a central and co-ordinating position. Nevertheless, your most hectic work is done before the class meets, and your traditional role of giving information to all your students simultaneously is certainly eroded. The emphasis shifts to the resources used, to the students themselves, and to the creative contributions they are able to make with your encouragement. In this way, too, the 'problem' of student participation melts away. Students participate as a matter of course because activity is built into the whole exercise.

Problems of resources

Every novelty in educational method brings with it some danger that devotees will recommend it as a cure-all for every classroom malaise. It is unlikely that any one method will be right for every class all that time, and this is as true of simulation, case studies and role play as of any other method. Role playing and simulation are not all plain sailing for teacher or learner. Although they are highly flexible methods and, once prepared, can be used with a variety of different classes, the preparation can be lengthy and exacting.

Emotional display

Tutors who have not used role playing and simulation tend to brood anxiously about the potential dangers of inviting too much emotional involvement from students. Adult classrooms generally tend to be peaceful places and you may hesitate before plunging your students into what might turn out to be an embarrassing emotional display.

It is for this reason, no doubt, that, of the four techniques described in this chapter, case study is by far the most commonly used, precisely because it allows emotional issues germane to the group to be discussed coolly at a distance in terms of other people's problems, but without any of the apparent hazards involved in role playing. It is true that in role playing some students may be alarmed by the passionate response a role play draws from them or from others. It is true that some role playing becomes nearly indistinguishable from the real thing. But in practice it is never quite the real thing, tempers never run quite so high, your emotions are never quite so fully engaged as they are in the real situation, because, however realistic the setting, the problem, or the incidental detail, you never forget that you are in a classroom. Particularly where the tutor has stressed that it is not their own but other people's roles that students are to play, there is always some sense of distance between action and thought. In a group which has become experienced in using the technique, there is a noticeable feeling that it is quite all right to indulge the emotions a situation may provoke because these emotions are in themselves valuable source material for the follow-up discussion and analysis.

Student anxieties

A more real difficulty, especially at first, is the opposite one that adult students may refuse to become involved at all, they may not wish to step out of the conventionally passive student role into something that seems to bear a suspicious resemblance to amateur dramatics. A student who is nervous about speaking in public may be even more embarrassed about role playing. This difficulty arises most often where role playing is used in academic subjects, when it will be most noticeably in conflict with traditional methods of teaching and where it probably grows less naturally and genuinely out of the work than out of subjects where the basic art being taught is skill in human relationships. A student who has enrolled for what looks like being a straightforward enough course in international relations may well feel as peeved about the introduction of academic gaming as the customer who finds that a comfortable, undemanding local pub has gone in for poetry readings. If role playing and simulation can only be introduced with a great fanfare and with much special pleading from you, then it is probably unsuited to the course. In any case, it is probably best tried gradually, without fuss and on a small scale at first.

Problems for the tutor

One of the reasons students may be suspicious of role playing and simulation is that they are not orderly, predictable methods of learning. There are no prepackaged maxims that can be transferred direct from tutor to learner. On the contrary, students not only have to elaborate on a given situation by actively interpreting it, they then have to deduce the general rules for themselves. This is why the follow-up discussion is so important. It is also why learning through simulation, role playing and case study takes so much longer and is so much more diffuse and sprawling than a series of lectures. Use of these techniques, therefore, makes considerable demands on the tutor, not only in the time and skill they will demand in preparation, but also in your ability to train your groups to generalize a clear overall picture from a series of specific examples.

Perhaps the most common practical difficulty is that tutors are often unable to encourage the group to look beyond the rights and wrongs of a particular case. If the material is sufficiently intriguing, group members will sometimes argue it endlessly, but take it no further than that. If the material is less absorbing, they may tend to discuss it in a desultory way for a short time, but will then dismiss it by implying that because conditions in their job, school or locality are not exactly like the ones in the case study, there is nothing to be learnt from it. This can be a particularly pressing problem with people who have a narrow but extremely intensive practical knowledge of their own cases while rejecting the applicability of either general theory or other cases to their own.

A first necessary step might be for you to demonstrate through role play that even their own case looks different when seen from different angles, but progress here is bound to be slow. With such groups, case study, role play and simulation done badly is particularly frustrating for the students, who are understandably inclined in such circumstances to start muttering in favour of bringing back formal methods where at least the outward trappings of learning – talk and chalk, headings and subheadings – are familiar.

Another real enough shortcoming, particularly of case-study techniques, is that there is never as much information available as there would be in real life. Students will often criticize a slackly prepared case study on these grounds by saying that they cannot possibly argue the case without more information. I once sat in with a group of senior managers who were being invited to solve a problem based on a difficult business situation. Discussion was slow because the study itself had been too crudely drawn. In the end the group decided that the only way their discussion could be turned into something useful to themselves was for them to decide what extra information they would have needed in order to solve the problem. In real life there are, of course, often severe limitations to the amount of information that is available. Most tutors believe that case studies must and should omit confusing and conflicting detail, though some exponents of case-study and simulation techniques would stress that it is sometimes necessary to introduce this, too, to teach relevance and choice. But in general there must be simplification, not so much that the case is hopelessly falsified to the state where students will reject it, and never so complicated that it is beyond the current capacities of the group to solve. Where the case study is extended into role play some of this danger recedes because the case itself takes on the added dimensions which active participation must give.

Making role play work

In spite of all these problems, role play in particular is a uniquely valuable technique – superb at helping people learn behavioural skills. It is probably the only way, for instance, that you could train adequately as a Samaritan, because it is the only technique that could give you supervised practice before you are let loose in the real world, where an untrained Befriender would quickly feel confused and inadequate as well as being potentially quite likely to behave unhelpfully with clients. It is certainly the best way for shop assistants to learn how to deal with customers. A few stints of role-played practice at handling an aggressive customer are worth any amount of written advice in the staff manual. But, like any other technique, role play needs care in execution. Normally, you will need to work through all the following stages:

Objectives

Be clear about which objectives you are hoping to meet through role play. Write yourself a tightly defined brief before you begin. For instance, if you are thinking of running a role play on selection interviewing, it will probably not be helpful to think vaguely: 'Well, it will do them good to see it from the other person's point of view'. It will be better to write down something like: 'Having completed the role play, the participants should be able to list ten examples of open-ended questions, describe 'hostile' body language', and so on.

Choose or design appropriate material

To work with your group, the material must be relevant, brief and credible. If you are writing your own, then you may need to check it out with a suitable 'reader' first: one tiny error (for instance, a wrong job title) could destroy the 'willing suspension of disbelief' in your group as surely as it does to spot a continuity error in a film. It is always better to base a role play on a real situation if possible: this gives you the perfect reply to students who protest that such a scenario could 'never' happen, and is also likely to provide you with the small details and complexities that bring a case to life. But beware of 'scripting' a role play too lengthily or in a way that leaves little room for manoeuvre and elaboration. People may feel constrained by all the detail or simply refuse to take part: 'I'm just not like that person, I wouldn't behave like that.'

Introduce and explain the benefits of role play to the group

Role play may be new to many of your group and they will need time to consider its virtues and drawbacks. If you intend to use the technique then you will need to sell its benefits vigorously. Explain the difference between 'role play' and 'acting', and describe the normal progress of a typical role play. It usually helps to quote the comments of former students who may themselves have been dubious about it at the start but who ended up convinced of its merits.

Give a detailed briefing before you begin

The briefing is part of the learning because here you introduce the ideas the role play is designed to explore. Tell the group what your objectives are, what the 'rules' are about how much time is allowed, whether or not the players should confer in advance or consult you. This is also the stage to brief group members who are not 'playing' but observing. They should all have an 'observation sheet' which they fill in as the role play progresses. For instance, if they are to observe an 'annual assessment' between a 'manager' and a 'subordinate', then they could have a sheet which lists different behaviours which they tick or cross. Tell the observers what you expect them to do later – normally to give feedback to the players. Depending on the type of role play, you may like to give different observers different types of task – for instance one set could observe the 'manager' and one the 'subordinate'.

Run the role play

Keeping it brief has the virtue that several 'players' (say three pairs) can take part. Five minutes of role play will often generate twice as much discussion. Be prepared to step in if the role play wilts or becomes too intense or begins to ramble away from the main issue.

Debriefing

There is no point in role play without debriefing. It is the process of debriefing which helps make the learning points. It is often wise to let the role players have the first word. 'How did you think that went?' 'What did you think of the way you handled X?' 'How did it compare with the way you deal with this in real life?' Giving the role players this first chance to speak allows them to wind down and step back from the role. It also establishes a helpfully self-critical atmosphere.

Next, ask the observers for their feedback. You will already have established the same rules for sensitive and helpful feedback as you use yourself (see Chapter 4 for detailed hints on how to do this) but this process must be handled with infinite care, especially when people have been playing a role which is near to their own real circumstances and where it is reasonable to assume that they will therefore be extra-vulnerable to clumsily-offered negative feedback.

Now make the transition into a general discussion about underlying themes. These can be prepared in advance. Has the role play thrown up general trends or difficulties which parallel problems in the real world? Has it revealed insights (we hope that it has) into how similar issues may be handled 'for real'? What tends to get in the way of the 'ideal' solution?

Finally, don't forget to thank and praise the players for their efforts. This is important: many people will have taken part vigorously, but may privately wonder later if they have lost face by doing so. Forestall this reaction by making it clear that it is entirely thanks to their skill and commitment that such a valuable discussion was possible.

Refine the role play

Running a role play for the first time will usually reveal some flaws in its design. Regard the first run as a pilot; make suitable alterations in the light of useful comments from students or observations of your own.

Checklist on role play

Are your objectives in running the role play clear

- to you? ☐
- to your group? ☐

Is the role-play material

- relevant? ☐
- credible? ☐
- brief? ☐

Have you made detailed plans to brief

- the participants? ☐
- the observers (e.g., with an observation sheet)? ☐

Have you planned the appropriate time for

- initial briefing? ☐
- running the role play? ☐
- feedback from observers? ☐
- debriefing? ☐
- final wind-up? ☐

Have you prepared discussion points for the debriefing? ☐

10

Tutoring open learners

A tedious discussion at a recent conference I attended was a long and acrimonious wrangle about the differences between 'open' and 'distance' learning. It was tedious because these definitions are not particularly helpful to either 'experts' or learners. I shall use 'open learning' to describe any system where learners work alone, 'own pace, own place', on resources prepared by others, with minimal face-to-face contact either with tutors or other learners. Correspondence colleges provide such opportunities, as do the Open University, The Open College, the National Extension College and many colleges of further education. All have their own unique strengths and weaknesses which can be debated with theological fervour by cognoscenti. If you are involved as a tutor of open learners, these differences don't really matter. Much more will unite your clientele than will divide them.

Here, for instance, are some typical open learners:

- A young woman of seventeen on a YTS scheme run by a national retail chain. Her school record was not particularly distinguished. Now she is the only trainee in her shop, situated in a small East Anglian town. The 'modules' arrive from a college of further education in the North of England and she is expected to work through them alone except for certain 'exercises' which have to be done with the help of her line-manager at the shop. There are two residential weekends which are part of the course.
- A twenty-four-year-old graduate trainee working in a Bank. The company has bought 50 sets of an Open College course on Time Management. Four other trainees in the same area have started the course simultaneously. They meet every four weeks under the guidance of a tutor appointed by the Bank. All are expected to

submit work for a management qualification at the end of the course.

- A young trainee engineer at British Steel is using the company's own interactive video disc to acquire some basic skills, making regular visits to one of the company's own open learning resource centres.
- A sixty-year-old retired publican doing an Open College of the Arts course. She has always enjoyed 'arts and crafts'. This course is giving her a structured approach to painting and drawing.
- A thirty-four-year-old woman in her fourth year of an Open University arts degree course. She left school at eighteen with good A levels, but did not take up the offer of a university place. This course will, in her own eyes, prove her mettle and will help her find a job when her children are old enough to leave home. The summer schools are the highlight of her year.
- A twenty-nine-year-old woman working as an Accounts Assistant in a small company. She wants to become a certified accountant as this is the only way to improve her salary. The company has refused financial help with training, but she is willing to pay for herself, and has enrolled on two Open College–ACCA Level One Accountancy courses. Her job involves long hours and she is finding it tough to keep going both courses simultaneously, in spite of being advised against this by her tutor.
- A fifty-year-old woman working towards an A level in English through the National Extension College. Her motive is 'to acquire a decent certificate in a subject I've always loved'. She has never met her tutor – all their communication is on paper.
- A fifty-five-year-old man recently made redundant, now determined to set up his own business, working through an open learning Small Business course, recommended by the local Advice Service he has consulted. He has opted not to have a tutor at all, and is simply working through the course materials: two workbooks, two video tapes and an audio tape.

These people show something of the extraordinary range of open-learning opportunities now available. Open learning is no longer the specialized province of degree work or a narrow band of professional qualifications, both perhaps in the past regarded as second best choices and often as second rate into the bargain. Open learning is now joining the mainstream in an unfussed way as a perfectly normal choice for some people in some circumstances. Perhaps the employer doesn't have trainers on the payroll, perhaps there are too few people at any one time to train simultaneously, perhaps the trainees are geographically scattered. Perhaps people missed out on some aspects of their education in youth, or it may just be that changing times and circumstances have created a need for updating, training or academic study.

But however different their subjects or circumstances may be, there are many ways in which open learners are likely to feel the same about their work.

Disadvantages for students

Before the advent of the Open University, correspondence tuition was notorious for its high drop-out rate. Colleges not unnaturally tend to be shy on the subject, but we know that on some of the more demanding courses, as few as 10 per cent of the initial enrolment survived to take the final examination. Even all the skill and care of the Open University cannot prevent roughly half the intake failing to complete its degree courses. All this suggests that students do not find open learning easy.

Some students are not 'joiners' by temperament. They relish working alone. It is probably more common, however, to find that solitary learning needs unlimited quantities of self-discipline:

> I used to come home from work and set myself a target of two hour's studying. I was divorced by then so had no excuses. There was only me. However, there lay the problem. I found myself infinitely distractible. I'd jump up and play the piano, or glance at a magazine, or find my hand straying towards the knob on the television set, or start planning the meal for the next day. When I was a schoolchild I used to find it boring sitting in rows with other kids, but at least the teachers kept you at it . . .

The support of other students is an element taken for granted in face-to-face teaching. Its absence in open learning can matter even to the most fiercely motivated:

> Having missed out on proper higher education because of family problems I was absolutely determined to get what I felt I deserved through the Open University. I was completely ruth-

> less about my time and didn't find it too much of a problem to get in the number of hours I needed. Even so, I longed to discuss and talk with other people tackling similar assignments. I couldn't get very often to the study centre – it was nearly forty miles away and there was only one other student on the same course and I didn't rate my tutor too highly. One of the things that really sticks in my mind is taking a [study] unit to read on the long train journey to London once and spotting someone else with the same one! I was cheeky enough to introduce myself immediately and the time absolutely flew by. That was a real luxury: to talk science the whole time with a fellow student.

Working alone has other disadvantages: it tends to allow anxious students to become even more anxious. Adult learners are prone to nervousness anyway but in face-to-face teaching this can quickly be diminished both by sensitive teaching and by being with other students. In one wonderfully and unintentionally comic experiment, Pavlov, the distinguished Russian psychologist, found that if he performed a psychological test on a sheep, the mere presence of a second sheep made the first sheep less nervous. Common sense suggests that human beings are comforted in the same primitive way. A lone student easily develops a terror of showing his own real or imagined 'inadequacy'. It is common, for instance, for open learners to dread a tutor's judgement so much that they delay both starting and sending in their assignments. Many people spend two or three times the recommended number of hours on a piece of work, in painstaking and unnecessary reading and rereading. One of the Open University's first batch wryly commented:

> It's just as well I never have to admit the actual number of hours I spend on assignments. I'm sure I'd be told if I take the time I do I should never be taking the course.

That student spoke for hundreds of thousands of others subsequently whose experience was just the same.

Even in the classroom it takes all a tutor's skill and sensitivity to find the right ways of reassuring nervous students. It takes even more delicacy where the main means of communication is written. Face to face, a tough criticism can be softened and made acceptable by the way it is delivered. A tutor in the classroom may literally take her student to one side, may smile, may put one protective arm round him and then say 'Really, Mr ____, this essay won't do!' Her tone will indicate that she means the professional criticism to stand, but the smile, the gesture, her stance – her 'body language' in fact – will convey that no personal insult is intended. The identical comment written baldly down on an essay will have a very different impact – indeed it would take an unusually tough and confident student to remain unscathed by it. Written comment of this type is at worst withering for the recipient, at best infuriatingly ambiguous. In the classroom, at least there is opportunity to challenge a judgement on the spot; this is much more difficult for the open learner.

For lower-level academic work the inevitable emphasis on reading and writing in open learning has other disadvantages. It means the student must already be reasonably skilled and reasonably confident of his ability to cope with his own written work and with books:

> I can't describe the sweat of doing that first piece of work. I'd written reports – brief ones – but proper writing like this I hadn't attempted since I was fifteen. After working on it for hours I showed it to my wife and she said it was fine. I looked back on it later and I was amazed how tactful she'd been, but I can tell you this, no piece of work I did later cost me so much in time and effort. And it was only half a page!

In some ways anxiety is likely to be worse the more highly motivated and able the student. Few adults undertake a demanding piece of learning 'for the sake of the subject'. Many want to learn skills which they can apply in their daily lives. Where open learning is concerned, one dominant motive may be the wish to gain a qualification. For some people, of course, this is simply a necessary and inevitable step in their career development. For many more, however, it is a way of providing their worth to themselves and to others:

> I am a housewife with three young children and typical of so many I suppose in that I felt my brain stopped working when I had my first child. I did the course to prove to my husband and his friends that I was not just a meal-provider and nappy changer. It did them (and me) and the children so much good to see me sitting at a desk with books. It was very hard going and

> very lonely at times as I had to give up my local class. I worried terribly about failing, as that would have been thoroughly mortifying. I just had to get that O level after telling everyone I was doing it.

Adults, like this student, prefer open learning because it allows them to fit their academic work around their other commitments. But this, too, can create problems if the course becomes so intensely involving that pressures build up too much for comfort. There is a limit to the number of potatoes which can be peeled while simultaneously reading a set book; there is a limit past which lunch hours cannot be stretched to rough out assignments. Open learners frequently become over-tired and over-stressed as a result. Some women, for instance, may start a guilty frenzy of extra housework to prove to their families that domestic life will go on yet more perfectly than before; some people may simply find both academic and other commitments utterly overwhelming and may make a mess of both.

Isolation, anxiety and a failure to control the pace of work successfully are particular problems with those open learners who have not undertaken a substantial piece of learning for some time. They tend to have lost (or sometimes never to have acquired) the skills of studying. They may, therefore, spend hours reading every word of a book which only needs to be scanned: they may attempt laborious verbatim recording where sketchy notes would be more appropriate. In face-to-face teaching you can spot such problems and take remedial action. Where the bulk of the learning must be conducted through written material these difficulties may remain submerged, to the point where tutor and student alike become discouraged and defeated.

Some open learning involves broadcasting, but this continues to be a mixed blessing. The Open College tends not to use its programmes for 'teaching', only for 'motivating', whereas the Open University has built a substantial slab of didactic teaching into its broadcast programmes.

These media bring advantages. Students will have a second chance to understand complex material because it must inevitably be presented in a different way. Television can usually show a scientific demonstration more vividly than it can be described in a book; real drama can enliven a dull novel. Academic debate may become more gripping when the passion of the participants can be seen and heard rather than just read.

Nevertheless, broadcasting poses problems when it is involved in open learning. Perhaps most importantly, students (and tutors, too) may find the programme difficult to 'use'. This is particularly so with television, which most of us watch entirely for relaxation. Many students find it unexpectedly taxing to acquire the different frame of reference which may be needed to watch an educational television programme. They will perhaps be irritated by an academic presenter who is full of the distracting mannerisms which are usually trained out of existence in general broadcasting; or, because they expect something 'educational' they may be baffled by the producer's choice of a case study which carefully avoids the neat structure and tidy conclusions of a lecture or essay, not realizing that it is meant to be viewed entirely as 'evidence' – contradictions, prejudices and all. A sophisticated response like this must be worked for: it does not come naturally.

For instance, in the 1970s, BBC Radio produced an O-level course called *Living Decisions in Family and Community*. They wrote in a deliberately one-dimensional soap opera family called the Clarkes to exemplify conventionally delivered academic points about decision-making. As a device, the Clarkes tended to be unpopular with the audience. 'They are as repellent a family as I have ever heard', wrote one furious listener, maddened by their stereotyped dialogue. In general, particularly at the beginning of the course, people found it impossible to judge the Clarkes as illustrative ciphers. Students persisted in comparing the stories and the acting – usually unfavourably – with *The Archers*, or else in demanding their removal from the series altogether because they were a 'distraction' from the 'serious' business of learning.

Disadvantages for tutors

Most of the problems for students have their parallels for tutors. Tutors, too, tend to be isolated. They may also be undertaking open learning work because in theory it can combine with other commitments, yet find in practice that it becomes very demanding. Such teaching is rarely lucrative, and it is much more difficult for the tutor to achieve one of the main satisfactions of the teacher's job: getting to know students and to observe their development. Accurate diagnosis of a student's difficulties is often reduced to guesswork when the only clues are written ones. Conventional teaching, even to tightly organized syllabuses, also usually allows teachers an enormous degree of freedom to develop their own materials and methods. In open learning this freedom is largely absent. The materials, the marking system, the methods, will already have been laid down. In some ways, the more efficient, caring and conscientious the system, the less impact individual tutors will be allowed to have on it. This cry from the heart is made by Pauline Kirk, a part-time tutor for the Open University:

> I find myself affected by an increasing intellectual loneliness. My work for the Open University takes up so much of my time and energy, yet who knows, apart from my students? If I grade out of line the computer will pick up my aberration, or if I write too few comments my staff tutor will phone me tactfully, but in neither case will a central academic understand or care. I am infinitely replaceable . . . the part-timer's teaching duties are regarded merely as the assessment of, and support for, a centrally designed programme . . . In the Open University, then, one has a situation unique in British education – the existence of a large part-time teaching proletariat and a small academic ruling class.*

Advantages

In spite of all these difficulties, the benefits of open learning for both tutor and student are considerable. First, the learner is at the centre of the action. The best open learning materials will involve the students 'internalizing' a uniquely-tailored 'package' which is a close match to his or her circumstances. The learner controls the pace: for instance, an Open College thirty-hour course can be done in one intensive week, if you really want to, or spread over a year if that suits you better: you are not forced to keep time with other people. Even the apparent 'loneliness' of learning may have its appeal. Initial (unpublished) research done in early Open College days showed a large number of those questioned who had a strong

* Pauline Kirk, 'The loneliness of the long-distance tutor', *Teaching at a Distance*, no. 7, Open University Press, 1976.

preference for learning alone and a positive distaste for the company of other students or human teachers. The best open learning materials will offer learners the best there is, the most up-to-date theories, the liveliest minds, and a commitment to interactivity which would put much face-to-face teaching to shame. The materials are portable and can fit in with other responsibilities. Work for my own OU course was done as often on buses and trains or in the office as it was in a quiet room at home.

With vocational courses there is a further advantage: you are not cocooned from 'reality' while studying. Indeed 'reality' will probably be an important part of your course: important, for instance, in management training where many people have found that resolutions made on training courses to turn over new leaves begin to fade when back with all the demanding distractions of the real world.

Judging the quality of the course

Before committing yourself as a tutor of open learners, you may want to think carefully about the quality of the materials. A poor set of course materials can put you in the invidious position of having to endorse a product of which you disapprove. Better to scrutinize the course in advance and, if you dislike it, to decline the offer to work on it rather than to find yourself undermining the learners' motivation by subtle sniping or faint praise.

Good-quality open learning materials will usually have all the following features:

- Objectives written in testable and 'behavioural' terms (i.e. expressed as things the learner will be able to *do* closely linked to the skills needed for the task).
- Objectives stated for each unit or subsection.
- Simple, direct language which avoids sexist or racist stereotypes.
- An interactive style where the learner constantly has to contribute answers to 'problems', carry out tasks and projects, draw up action plans, supply personal interpretations and solve puzzles.
- Variety in the tasks the learner is asked to complete.
- 'Answers' which oblige the learner to draw on his own experience.
- Feedback on the learner's 'answers'.

- High-quality professional design: large print, pleasing use of white space, colour and illustrations; enough space to write 'answers' comfortably; ability to open the workbooks flat.
- Material presented in 'timed' chunks of not longer than two hours.
- Assessment (e.g. self-assessment questions) closely linked to the objectives.
- A summary at the end of each unit.
- A course index.
- Sturdy binding and packaging.
- Variety in and appropriate use of media: print alone *may* be enough, but some audio-visual variety is usually both desirable and necessary. Audio, video and Computer Based Training (CBT) should be professionally made and well matched to the print.

There is now much open learning material available which triumphantly meets all these criteria. However, there is also an awful lot of which does not. I was once proudly shown a text by a company which claimed it produced excellent open learning materials. The pages on display were already leaking out of a ring binder which was too small, and looked just like a set of lecture handouts. I commented mildly that it didn't look much like open learning to me. 'Ah', they said, 'but look, there's plenty of white space at the top and bottom of the pages!' White space at the top and bottom of the page is most definitely not what quality open learning is all about.

Apart from visual dullness and lack of professionalism in design, there are two other common flaws in poor-quality open learning material. One is the failure to realize that every word must count. Many producers give in to the temptation to write lengthy bookish paragraphs. It should be impossible to skim-read an open-learning text; it should be designed to be 'worked through', not 'read'. The other common flaw is pitching the language at the wrong level – normally too high for the target audience. Sometimes this is because the authors wish to pander to what they see as the academic snobbery of those who have commissoned them; sometimes it is a straightforward failure to realize that many people will simply be baffled by the casual and unexplained use of words like, for instance, 'andragogy' or 'transmogrification' (both of those words I encountered recently in open-learning courses allegedly aimed at people with no higher education).

The task of tutoring

In conventional teaching, as a conscientious tutor you will try to develop a whole battery of skills: those of the teaching methods specialist, group manager, resource manager, counsellor, subject specialist, setter and evaluator of work. It is this formidable array of roles which makes teaching such an extraordinarily complex and demanding job. Most open learning tutoring, however, requires both less and more than this. Of course, tutors must be specialists in their subjects, but most of your efforts must be concentrated on developing the skills of counselling and evaluation. Furthermore, these must be practised in written form. This is not at all the simple matter it may appear to teachers used to scrawling a few hasty marginalia on the scripts of students they also see face-to-face. Open learners, with all the disadvantages described earlier in this chapter, are peculiarly vulnerable to ill-considered written comment but are at the same time usually well able to judge the quality of a tutor's evaluative skill, as these quotes show:

> My comments this year have been extremely short, have criticised me on points specifically raised and no others and have thus been frustratingly useless. . . . I feel comments should be made not just on a personal basis e.g. 'surely not *that*', or 'dynamic' underlined and 'natural' put in, but on a more general level too – about *doing* literary criticism and how I could specifically improve my work and my grades.

> First of all I look for encouragement, this always give me a boost to do better! I look for constructive criticism and keep this in mind to work from. I would always readily appreciate a more general criticism showing plainly if I was taking the wrong approach to the studies, or the specific question. I feel that this kind of help could quite possibly save a student a whole year's work.*

What, then, is the best strategy to follow? The extremes are easily avoided. Few tutors would need to be told that it is inexcusably arrogant, not to say vituperative, to write 'You are suffering from

* Two Open University students, quoted in Kenneth MacKenzie, 'Student reactions to tutor comments on the tutor-marked assignment', *Teaching at a Distance*, no. 5, Open University Press, 1976.

intellectual paralysis', as indignantly reported by one student. Nor would many fall into the opposite trap of the tutor who said ruefully of her own performance:

> I am so terrified of apparently giving insults that I hardly dare write anything critical. My marks are always too high until exams loom up – then I panic. I know it's not fair but I'm afraid of hurting my students by 'honest' criticism.

Basic guidelines for giving open learners feedback

The basic guidelines have to be much the same as for giving away feedback in learning (see Chapter 4). The only difference is that much of it (perhaps all) has to be given in writing and every word must be weighed because that is what will happen to it when it is received by your learners.

- *Praise the positive first.* 'You have really understood the main points that Units 1 and 2 are making . . .'.
- *Keep it objective.* 'It might be better to have started the Assignment with your second paragraph as this has much more "punch"' is better than 'I didn't like your opening paragraph'.
- *Be specific, be clear; give reasons* for praise or criticism. Wherever possible, comment should be full and unambiguous. There is no place in open learning for the inscrutable ticks, mysterious interrogatives and baffling exclamation marks which may appear on a script, whose author the tutor will see in the classroom. Allusive comments are also unhelpful. Face to face, you can explain what you meant by the cryptic words 'Jane Austen!' or 'Tawney!' in the margin. An open learner will all too probably be left guessing.
- *Let the student work it out.* Comments like 'You should have done this experiment in a different order: stage B should have preceded stage 'A' are misguided. Prescriptive feedback merely undermines learners' needs and probably their wishes, too, to work out the 'answer' for themselves. You already know the 'answer': they must come to it by themselves. It would be better to write 'Look again at the order in which you did this experiment and compare with Unit 4. Stage B in your "answer" is the key.
- *Give feedback quickly.* Return assignments within a few days:

the effort will be fresher in the learner's mind and your comments will therefore have more impact.

- *Keep it succinct and appropriate.* Your own experiences, quotes from theories at a much more advanced stage . . . these are all distractions. Stick to the main points.
- *Be restrained with negative criticism.* Students need to have straightforward factual errors corrected in their work. A mistaken response is in any case harder to eradicate from an adult's than from a child's mind and the sooner it is put right the better. Even so, a page which comes back disfigured by a smallpox rash of negative red markings is horribly discouraging; it is always better to refer learners to the original sources which they can then check for themselves. When a student's work is persistently full of factual errors this always calls for investigation: perhaps he has short-term special difficulties, perhaps he needs intensive remedial teaching, perhaps he should not be on the course at all.

As with all good teaching, you must show that you understand and identify with the student's point of view. A tutor who with strident triumph writes 'No! No! No!' on a student's work shows insensitivity as well as bad manners. Adult students are both easily put down by such comment and also inclined after an interval to reassert their own values and self-confidence: in other words, no learning can take place from such a negative exchange.

More subtly than this, you need to write comments which deliberately acknowledge that you have absorbed what the student was trying to achieve. For instance, 'I see that you have thoroughly read X's book and I agree with your comments on his general theories. However, when you come to Z I think you should reread his section on Y where you may come to the conclusion that . . . Most authorities feel that . . .'. A tone like this, which perhaps seems at first contrived and tentative, nevertheless allows the student to retain his self-esteem, flatters by showing that the tutor has taken him seriously and yet still allows space to reconsider the original judgement. Genuinely friendly, open and hesitant comments which do not appear to close off further discussion have another advantage, too. They may allow both tutor and student to elevate their relationship to the status of an honest and absorbing dialogue, a continuing conversation rather than the snap and crackle of a boss–

subordinate relationship, with all the resentful or craven submission that usually involves. Students who are on the receiving end of closed comments may also start trying to perform to rule, by simulating the kind of approach they come to believe will keep the tutor satisfied. The learning people accomplish under such conditions is nearly always bogus since it has not truly engaged either their minds or their emotions.

On the other hand, tutors who can develop the true dialogue approach can refine it to considerable effect. Teachers rated 'outstanding' by their students have at least one quality in common – they convey an ebullient and infectious enthusiasm for their subject which in itself is a tremendous stimulus to students. This quality is rare and it takes skill to convey that creative zest through words. Nevertheless, it can be achieved, as shown in this quote from an NEC student, who wrote admiringly of her tutor:

> She never overwhelms you with new concepts, but her great gift is to tempt you with some dazzlingly interesting thought/book/newspaper article just at the time you're most ready to accept it. She gives the impression that she lives, breathes and sleeps her subject. I so look forward to getting my work back – it's like getting a particularly challenging and interesting letter from a friend now!

- *Be prepared to look underneath specific difficulties for underlying problems.* Spotting symptoms is easy, knowing the cause is far more demanding. Students who naively copy out whole paragraphs from a set text without acknowledgement may not be unintelligent, devious or foolish. They may just be ignorant of the academic conventions of quotation. Students who have clearly only consulted one out of several suggested sources for an essay may not be either lazy or stupid. They may simply not know how to gut a book quickly.

How much you can help with such problems depends to some extent on how much your employing organization can tell you about the learner. Most will supply you with the learner's biography and will expect you to send a matching one of your own to the student. You may be encouraged to make both telephone and face-to-face contact. If you are tutoring someone inside your own organization then much more may be possible.

You will certainly be expected to keep scrupulous records of progress, and may also be required to help learners negotiate a realistic timetable for completing assignments (though not in the Open University, where there is usually a set timetable for each course).

Any disadvantages of open learning are immeasurably offset by building in human support: through 'mentors', self-help groups, tutorials, summer schools and seminars. They mitigate the potential loneliness and anxiety, while at the same time maintaining all the immense pluses of putting the learner at the centre of the whole process. The skills involved in running such encounters are by and large the same as in other kinds of face-to-face teaching and are dealt with elsewhere in this book.

Checklist on open learning tutoring

Have you worked through the course materials to check on their quality? ☐

Has your personal contact with each learner involved:

- your receiving a biography from them? ☐
- their receiving a biography from you? ☐

Is the feedback you offer on written work

- positive? ☐
- objective? ☐
- specific? ☐
- possible to put into practice? ☐
- non-prescriptive? ☐
- returned within a few days? ☐
- succinct? ☐
- cautious with negative comments? ☐

Are you prepared to look underneath symptoms for causes? ☐

11

Projects

Project work has been around a long time in schools. From being something daring and innovatory it has now become almost a cliché, in many cases earning itself a bad name for being an excuse for the teacher to have a quiet nap while the children are tucked away in the library copying out half-digested pieces from encyclopaedias, doing individual projects on sixteenth-century armour or timber-framed-houses-through-the-ages.

In adult education, on the other hand, the project is still in its prime and as a means of learning by doing and of teaching by investigation has developed in different ways. Far from being the occasion for the feats of individual academic virtuosity which the school-type project encourages at its best and lamentably fails to encourage at its worst, the adult-education project has become a way for the individual to learn within the group and for the group to learn from the community.

It is at this point of contact with the community that the adult-education project has had its most significant impact. Project work usually involves the group leaving the cocoon of the classroom and venturing out to seek raw materials from local people, records or conditions. Even where the materials have not been local, but have involved the group in an intensive study of some foreign or national event, the result of the project, its end product, has often been in a form which involved offering something to the community – a book, an exhibition, a series of study walks, a play.

Scope of the project method

Two classic studies, both sociological and undertaken by adult-education classes in Nottingham and Basingstoke, show something of the characteristic scope and impact of the project method. In Nottingham a group of twenty students under the leadership of two tutors form the university, Ken Coates and Richard Silburn, made a study of the St Ann's district of the town, uncovering widespread material deprivation, desperately poor housing, low aspiration and poor educational achievement.* The group, which began as a normal course in sociology, turned itself over three years into a highly efficient research team as well as continuing, as an adult-education group, to learn a good deal at a high conceptual level about social class in general, poverty in general and sociology in general. One of the students, Rosalind Kent, describes the personal impact the work had on her:

> The area itself was ugly, dirty and depressing to work in and, on occasion, a little frightening. Having felt my way, one dark night, from an alleyway down a long backyard, I arrived to find the house derelict and, suddenly, the next-door neighbour shining a torch into my face and inquiring what I was up to.
>
> Some of the families I interviewed were living in conditions of extreme discomfort; rotten house fabric, ill-fitting draughty windows, very damp walls, outside toilets, no hot-water systems or bathrooms and overcrowding were common facts of life. One particular family I remember was afflicted with all these ills and the mother had to share a bedroom with the daughter as this was the only means of giving her any privacy. Another woman had nursed a dying husband under these conditions and without realizing that she was entitled to sickness benefits. . . .
>
> Of course, as our survey progressed so did the spirit of teamwork and *camaraderie.* This had nothing to do with the fact that our gathering-point after a strenuous evening's interviewing was often a strategic pub.
>
> After the interviewing was over, I was left with a sense of guilt, each time, on returning to my own cosy middle-class home. . . .†

* Ken Coates and Richard Silburn, 'St Ann's: poverty, deprivation and morale in a Nottingham community', Department of Adult Educatin, University of Nottingham, 1967.

† Rosalind Kent, 'Not for ostriches', *WEA News*, March 1968.

The sense of indignation and surprise in this description, typical of the way the group and the tutors felt about what they were learning, was bound to seep through the apparently neutral, unemotional and well-illustrated report the group produced. The local impact was tremendous. Some members of the Council felt that what the group had uncovered was bound to be interpreted as an assault on their policies and efficiency. The group was attacked, often abusively, for seeming to be snoopers, or for exaggerating; other local people felt some of the outrage the group itself had felt about conditions in St Ann's, and were disturbed at the implications of the report. However the survey results are interpreted, it is surely right that a local community, and indeed a national one, should be aware of and should discuss something so important as the possibility of there being extensive poverty in its midst, and right also that the question can be raised by a group of people from the community itself who are at the same time engaged in serious learning within and through it.

In Basingstoke, on a less combustible subject, the WEA was involved almost from the start in plans to expand the town from being a small market town 26,000 strong to an overspill giant of 85,000. Starting in 1960, a series of classes studied and obtained new facts about innumerable aspects of the town's character, pouring out a stream of information at all sorts of levels, some of it aimed at academics engaged in town expansion and planning problems elsewhere, some of it amusing lighthearted reading, some simply designed to keep local people informed of developments, to prepare them for the future and to invite them to participate in planning it.

Projects have long tentacles. A WEA class in Herefordshire and Shropshire studying Offa's Dyke offered back some of its knowledge in the form of public 'summer-study walks', gave talks to branches of local archaeological societies, ran coach excursions, and became involved in negotiations to reopen rights of way over those parts of the Dyke which had become impenetrable jungles. An Offa's Dyke Action Committee was formed, maps of routes were made and distributed, guidebooks were written for people who wished to follow the routes. It is often the case that when, after such projects, the class itself has been wound up, and the members have learned a considerable amount of archaeology or sociology, the effectiveness of the work is continued by formation of a local pressure group or society. Much of the detailed archaeological and social history of

Britain has been rediscovered by groups of this type, which had their origin in an adult-education group which had stepped outside the self-absorption of the conventional class.

In all these projects the classes have not simply been the cheap, amateur means of making a survey, necessarily a form of sociological self-help in less centralized, sparsely populated parts of Australia or the United States. They have also been a serious method of learning for members of the groups, who through active involvement have perhaps been able to grasp tougher academic nettles than a class covering the same ground in a more passive way.

Opportunities for learning

Groups engaging on project work are as likely as members of other adult classes to be mixed in ability, confidence and experience. Project work, expertly managed, seems uniquely well suited to allow such members of the group to find their own level quietly at first, and then to seize opportunities for learning which might have seemed to present formidable obstacles if demanded of the same students in a conventional class. In theory there might be the danger that a few confident and assertive members of the group engage for themselves all the more 'interesting' tasks and surge ahead while the rest of the group splashes round still in the shallows. In practice this does not often seem to happen. Tutors who have led groups working on projects will frequently remark that if the project grips the interest of the group, it seems only a matter of time before every member of it makes some quite startling leap forward. It could be the shy woman, apparently too timid to take part in the ordinary interviewing for a social survey, who suddenly volunteers to interview a notoriously prickly member of the local Council. It could be the even shyer class member who stays silent through almost every class meeting, but who accepts without question that he will lead a study walk around an old fortress which the group is excavating, or that he will take his share of the lecturing engagements which come the way of the class through the local interest which the project has aroused.

The opportunities which a project offers to work with the group, but as a free agent inside it, also seem to stimulate a surprising amount of individual academic initiative. For instance, in one group of day-release students, many of whom had done no formal academic work for fifteen years or more, several students on different occasions appeared in the class with papers prepared through the results of research they had undertaken entirely on their own initiative. One such piece was a detailed and scholarly appraisal of all known sources of information on local pits since the fourteenth century; another was survey of the history of the village since the Domesday Book which drew on over twenty separate original sources. The only previous pieces of written work either of these students had done were half-page accounts, clearly written with difficulty, of the state of wage negotiations in one coalmine.

Indeed, the whole tormented 'problem' of wringing 'written work' out of students fades away in the context of a project. It is not at all surprising that teachers often find it hard to persuade students to write essays. Children may accept with comparative docility that one of the ways of learning is to shape recently acquired knowledge into a 1,000-word form with paragraphs, a beginning, a middle and an end, which is then appraised by the teacher. It is not surprising that adults resist what must appear to be a stereotyped presentation, artificial in the context of an adult class which is not going to be examined in the essay form.

Written work is, of course, a valuable way of learning, but it is only one among many ways – discussing, listening, thinking – of sifting, constructing and presenting an argument, and it does not have to take the classical essay form. In the course of a project, most of the group members will at some time do an extended piece of writing, which could well be more taxing to them than any essay, but its shape might be a simple duplicated sheet containing a few terse highlights, the fruits of a long, detailed piece of research into local wills, parish records and electoral registers, or it might be a paper formally written after an extensive reading programme and then delivered to the rest of the group, giving a god's-eye view of all the major academic writing on, say, Roman Britain or social class.

The difference between this sort of work and the normal essay is that students approach it for a different purpose. The delights of writing a good essay are normally the private and individual sense of pleasure produced by having tidied one corner of knowledge to one's own satisfaction. The motivation and reward are confined to this perhaps ritualistic transaction between teacher and student. With written work produced as part of a project there is the additional spur that it is being produced out of necessity: the rest of the group really needs to know what one has discovered. A piece of entirely new information or a cogent survey of other people's information, researched and assessed on one's own for this purpose, takes on an altogether different flavour, because the need to communicate it to other people is more intense.

Varieties of method

Then, too, the end product itself, and the very fact that there is to be an end product, may well mean that each member of the group has to produce more written work, and to a higher standard, than might be demanded in a conventional class. Some tutors write up the final report themselves, or the task may be undertaken completely by one or more members of the group. The procedure, like the form of the report itself, will depend on the group and on the task. Some reports have been duplicated sheets stapled together, distributed at a nominal price. Others have been simple pamphlets, but beautifully printed and illustrated.* The format need not be stereotyped. Indeed one major survey may be a fruitful and continuous source of varied end-product material – handouts, printed pamphlets, books, lectures and films, or even a documentary novel with several authors. The Basingstoke WEA's involvement in the plans for the town has among other things meant the production of a cheap pamphlet containing a collection of lighthearted quotations about the town, 'The Things They Say about Basingstoke'; a short pamphlet reporting on facilities in the town, 'Basingstoke – A Social Study'; a solid academic case study of town expansion, *Economic Planning and Town Expansion* by John Dunning, one of the teachers who led the group;† and a history of the town prepared as a tape-slide presentation, with a commentary spoken by John Arlott, which has already been lent out to audiences totalling well over 5,000 people.

It is a pity that this last type of enterprise is still so rare. Maybe it is the long years of fretting over the quantity of their students' written work, maybe it is the still-prevalent belief that the printed word is somehow superior to the spoken or recorded word, but most groups have chosen print for their end products. Admirably professional and thorough though most of these have been, it seems a pity that

* For example, *Hatfield and its people*, 12 vols, Hatfield WEA, 1959–64.
† John Dunning, *Economic Planning and Town Expansion*, Southampton WEA, 1963.

more adult groups have not also experimented with film, with drama (improvised or carefully written and rehearsed), or with video. Expense might preclude elaborate film and video work, but improvised drama certainly need not be costly, and facilities for sound recording are within every group's grasp. Indeed, now that there are so many local radio stations all eager for material, radio programmes will be perhaps the most natural way of communicating the first findings of a project group.

The more varied the forms of presentation, the more opportunities and challenges it will offer the members of the group for learning. Someone whose written work is poor may yet make a superbly informal and articulate radio presenter; the person who may not be entirely happy working on academic research may have a flair for its accurate and readable presentation in short articles for the local press. Other members of the group may have the creative skills in artwork or photography, invaluable in preparing material for printing or in mounting an exhibition.

Using existing skills

In this way projects offer not only the opportunities for developing new skills but also the chance to utilize old ones for the benefit of the group. Much noise is made in adult education about something normally known as 'using the experience and talents of the student', but it is rare for a teacher to be able to do very much more than simply offer concepts to the group for them to sieve through their own experience. Many of the generalizations, for instance, of sociologists and historians rightly prove too coarse for the exacting judgements made by members of adult classes, who are often less ready to accept such generalizations than young students. Teachers and students can feel happy that in these circumstances the student's life experience has been 'used' to the satisfaction of both. This is, of course, a valuable educational process as well as a courtesy due to adults by right. However, in a project, the student's professional skills as well as his general experience can become absolutely vital to the group. Here, for instance, in an extract from a paper by two Nottingham tutors, Coates and Silburn, is an example of how the composition and character of the class and the skills of its individual members affected the work the Nottingham group was able to do in its investigation of the St Ann's district.

When the class assembled in October, it had attracted twenty registrations, including a number of people with a professional interest in the chosen area, some of whom had access to facts, records and statistics which are not generally available. There were three probation officers, a schoolteacher who was married to an immigrant and who lived on the border of the area, an accountant in the corporation's housing department, two journalists, a charge-hand in a local factory who also served on its sick and benevolent fund committee, three secretarial employees, an architect in the employ of the city council, an accountant in private employment, and a number of housewives. Many of these people were able to set up separate but parallel investigations into the records of their own departments, thus producing a number of related profiles of the chosen area. Thus we obtained precise records of juvenile offenders in the area, of youth-club facilities of houses in the area which were owned by the corporation, of rateable values of industrial and commercial establishments within the area, and of some of the major complaints about overall living conditions within it. Other investigations whose results were keenly awaited included a detailed study of the educational needs of the area, and of the attainments of its children.

Other students who had not the advantage of access to otherwise restricted information were nonetheless able to make significant contributions to our knowledge of the area: for instance, one student completed a detailed survey of inward and outward mobility, street by street, from electoral registers chosen at an interval of four years. A number of students examined and priced the diet set out by Rowntree and Lavers in their classic *Poverty and the Welfare State*, revealing very wide discrepancies between price levels in city-centre supermarkets and local corner shops, to the considerable disadvantage of the corner shops. One keen student even went so far as to feed her family on the Rowntree and Lavers 1951 diet for a week, during which time they ingested not only a fair quantity of sago and lentils, but also six pounds of swedes. She reported that they were all relieved when the experiment was successfully concluded.*

* Ken Coates and Richard Silburn, 'Urban renewal: a social survey', *Adult Education*, vol. 40, no. 3, 1967.

The interdisciplinary factor

Much lip-service is paid today to the value of interdisciplinary studies, but the majority of tutors continue, understandably enough, to plough their lonely geographical, historical or literary furrows. To do anything else may be too time-consuming and simply too difficult for one person alone. One of the strengths and at the same time, of course, one of the potential weaknesses of project work is that such narrowness is virtually impossible. Because the findings themselves are by definition unknown to the teacher as well as to the group, there is no knowledge to be neatly parcelled up and presented in isolation. As soon as a group starts work on a project the boundaries of knowledge inevitably split and become blurred. For instance, a rural group whose members begin by studying local history, involving as they think the medieval church, the wool trade and the later local industries, might very well find themselves driven to looking as well at geography and geology to explain how it was that the wool trade grew up in the first place. They might also need to know some natural history to examine the ecological structure of the area, some archaeology to have a closer look at local remains, some demography to seek explanations of change in population, to say nothing of sociology when it came to comparing the past with the present.

Even a simple sociological project will most probably involve practising the social skills of interviewing, the literary skills of presenting information in agreeable form, as well as reading up the appropriate historical and literary background. The interdisciplinary skills acquired are not always intellectual ones. As part of one project an archaeological group felt obliged to build a medieval kiln in which they experimented with the production of thirteenth- and fourteenth-century glazed wares, while another group found and rebuilt an early steam engine as part of an investigation in industrial archaeology.

The larger view

One of the potential dangers of a project is undoubtedly that the group can bury itself so deep in local or intensively small issues that it can overlook the large ones, or fail to see where the links between local and national, minor and major developments can be made. It is clearly the tutor's job to see that these links are made in a sensible way. Some projects have begun because the groups themselves had failed to understand the large picture, or else simply did not believe it – the Nottingham group, for instance, started with a course on the 'Anatomy of Britain', and only found it a credible idea that 7.5 million people in Britain could be living in virtual poverty when they began to investigate the poverty on their own doorsteps. It was natural, then, in this survey for the group to be constantly driven back to the national picture as a yardstick for their local one. Such information needed to be acquired more urgently than it might have been in a class which had continued as a course of lectures. A class in this situation can accept a far more rigorous academic treatment, either from its own teacher or from a visiting specialist, than the constantly boiled-down fare it might more usually be offered, where the temptation to regurgitate received opinions and fifth-hand information is often too strong for a teacher to resist.

Furthermore, there is tremendous value in the process of having been involved themselves in making knowledge: sifting opinions, constructing questionnaires, excavating archaeological sites, examining documentation, searching through other people's arguments and then constructing an argument oneself. This gives students an altogether different way of looking at other people's work. The student who has himself helped construct a survey will know how important the phrasing of questions in the interview can be, and will be alert to the non-neutral words or leading questions in other questionnaires, whether these are in newspaper opinion polls or in the more extensive and weighty work of the academic sociologist. Someone who has herself struggled with untidy and sporadically available documentation will be aware of the historian's temptation to cover up the blank patches with words. The student who has been, if only for a short time, a craftsman-academic, handling the raw materials of history, sociology, geology or ecology, will inevitably see the structure of another craftsman's work more clearly than he would had he remained only an onlooker, however well informed.

Extra demands

These are joys for the students who survive the course. Undoubtedly many students find project work altogether too demanding, and once they discover what is involved, may drop out altogether. Work on a project cannot be tidily confined to two hours in one place once a week. It makes demands on time and money which many students will feel they cannot meet. A group investigating the recent past of their own geographically small area, at present the most simple and commonly undertaken project, will still find that plenty of time is needed for the leisurely interviews with old people with long memories who can recall the 'tyrant' at the big house – or other living detail which will bring a local history alive. Money may be needed for travelling, for buying reference books, for postage. It is unusual to find organizations generous enough to supply this kind of support, so that it may fall to students to pay these perhaps quite sizeable expenses themselves. The work itself, fascinating at the outset, or in its larger aspects, will undoubtedly have a tedious and dreary side when time is absorbed by ploughing through census returns or coding questionnaires for the computer, when 'real' results seem far away.

In a group working well, the growing sense of fellowship and group feeling produced by working towards a common goal will usually be sufficiently strong to carry students over the difficult patch where academic or personal energies seem to be flagging. In other groups this may be the moment when the whole project seems endangered and the tutor must perform some sort of inspirational rescue job.

The tutor's skills

Here, as throughout the work, the tutor's role is a vital, delicate and exhausting one. You have most certainly abdicated from any pedagogic dominance. In your occasional lectures given to fill in background or to introduce a new part of the project, you will be listened to respectfully, possibly with more attention but certainly with more critical scrutiny than before; you will have become in a noticeable way the servant of the group rather than its master. A group working on a project will quickly gain confidence from close familiarity with the raw material; the sum of students' local knowledge will be greater, and usually more intimate than yours as tutor, however well informed you keep yourself of work in hand.

You must know the abilities of your students and be aware of their friendships and antipathies. People work best when encouraged to work with their friends. A tutor who is ignorant of the particular bonds between students, or who deliberately and despotically sets out to destroy old bonds and create new ones, will surely wreck the project or weaken its effectiveness. Similarly, there is no point in attempting to force students to undertake work which seems to them at first grandiose or alarming. People who are frightened by the idea of tasks such as conducting interviews or coping with medieval documents should not be jollied or shamed into attempting them; instead, you should try to keep the channels of opportunity open, so that, if and when the less confident students change their minds, it is possible for them to do so at any time without loss of face. You should in any case try to prevent the growth of the situation seen in some project groups where some tasks come to seem humble and some important. Working in pairs rather than individually is one way round this problem, and it also overcomes the initial anxiety some students may feel that they are not capable of doing well whatever job they have been allotted. With someone else to share the responsibility, the possibility of 'letting the group down' or 'failing' the tutor in some way does not seem so frightening.

The majority of projects so far produced by groups both in Britain and in the United States have been of a sociological, archaeological or historical kind, and have involved groups in work lasting at least one and frequently three or more years. These protracted time-scales and apparently limited subject areas have been a disincentive to tutors in other subjects with less time at their disposal. There is, however, no reason why more modest work could not be attempted, some of it of an individual nature within a group, some of it short-term work for the whole group. Some starts have already been made. Two members of a WEA group studying local dialects in Staffordshire produced a pamphlet on children's rhymes, games and jokes; a group studying natural history who began with lectures but who wanted to test their knowledge in practice used part of their spring and summer sessions to make a census of breeding birds in one town.

Possibilities in adult education

So far most of the work has been done by single classes under a university or WEA flag, but it could be undertaken equally often and with equal efficiency by local authority classes, or by several classes working as a team with a number of tutors. A class working on car maintenance might well be involved at some time in a town-planning traffic survey, and might work together with a group studying architecture or sociology; a language class might make a feasibility study of a 'twinning' link between the town and a foreign city, working together with a local history group; an industrial relations class might engage on an examination of a local labour problem and draw in members of management training courses or classes studying economics and law.

The project itself need not necessarily be local or stereotyped in form. Some of the most striking work of this kind, admittedly done within the structure of full-time art education, was produced by the talented Albert Hunt at Bradford. Working with groups for a fortnight at a time his students have, for example, investigated the raid on Dresden; invented and then played children's games; researched the life of the murderer Christie; researched then rehearsed the details of the Cuban missile crisis; and explored themes such as incarceration. Some of these projects have been written up by students, some have been the basis of improvised theatre, in some the students felt that the experience was the sort where no formal end product was appropriate – the fortnight's work must simply be absorbed and pondered individually and left at that.

However, projects are not panaceas. There is no point in embarking on a survey if someone else has already produced a more than adequate one in the recent past. A project will no more inevitably save a dull class than it will engage the energies and attentions of a lively one. Projects are not miraculous teaching techniques to be produced out of a hat, but a means to serve educational and possibly social ends, and to be employed, therefore, with proper caution and respect.

Many adventures into project work have proved fruitful. Their early success spurred many organizers into arranging local history or 'trace-your-ancestors' groups after their original 'educational' remit had been fulfilled:

> I was persuaded to join an oral history group. It forged ahead and the first year we took part in a Living Memory exhibition held at the Festival Hall. The second year we entered a competition run by London Weekend TV in conjunction with their *The Making of Modern London* series. We got a very nice certificate for that.

Then in 1986 Camden Council appointed a co-ordinator of oral history groups in the borough for one year and as we were the only group meeting on a regular weekly basis, we had his services every week. He taught us a lot, how to record our sessions and interview each other. None of us was familiar with a tape-recorder: I had never handled one since the days when my boss had used a Ferrograph.

In 1987 we entered a second LWT competition and this time we won a runners-up prize of £100 which was presented at a grand 'do' at LWT headquarters. Currently the group is being filmed by Thames TV for a short series on oral history and we are currently working on an exhibition for the community centre Open Day in July and one for our local library. We are also hoping to visit one of the local primary schools to talk about the Second World War. We have already been to a girls' school in Hampstead who were doing a project and wanted to question us on all kinds of aspects, particularly the role of women. And one of the nicest things that has happened to us this year has been the visits made by a sixth-former from a local school which encourages its seniors to go into the community – she chose us and it was delightful to have her. She initiated one of the most interesting sessions we have had on the attitudes to women at work, asking some very pertinent questions.

And what of the future? Well, we are always working on something and one day, fairly soon we hope, we will be producing a booklet on the group's reminiscences about the area in which we live. We will be entering the next Living Memory Exhibition, and who knows, maybe someone else will want us to take part in a television series.

Making group projects work

Summing up, there are a number of steps that you can take to make sure the success of projects with a group:

- *Relevance*. The reason for doing the project must seem relevant and worthwhile.
- *Honesty*. Some projects have failed because the tutor's real reasons for organizing them have been covertly political. The intrinsic dishonesty of this motive has been quickly rumbled by

the group, and the project has collapsed. There is no reason why such a project could not be carried out successfully – as long as the banner under which it is organized is clearly stated.

- *Research skills*. Most groups will need to learn the basic skills of raw research: how to write a questionnaire, how to interview, how to use local archives. Successful organizers tend to help people acquire these technical aptitudes early on in the life of the project as a formal and deliberate part of the programme.
- *Resources*. Project work virtually always needs funding. Draw up a realistic budget and bid in advance for the extra cash from the sponsoring organization (if the Education Authority refuses to pay, there may be other sources of local funding: trusts, businesses, Arts Associations, and so on).
- *Time limits*. It is probably sensible to draw up a detailed schedule of all the important milestones you envisage for the project. They can be changed and discussed as you work through, but without targets the group may drift and will ultimately find its work unsatisfying.
- *Fair shares*. Keep scrutinizing the group to test its temperature and to see who is doing what. Be alert to signs that one person (or more likely, one little clique) is dominating in a way that is causing resentment among the others. The best 'cure' will be up to you, but you have the usual possibilities at your disposal: they will range from bluntly ordering the behaviour to cease at one end of the spectrum, to discussing the 'problem' and consulting the group at the other.
- *Objectives*. Whether *you* design the brief, evolve it with the group, or design an outline brief which is then discussed is up to you: there is something to be said for all these options. However, one way or another there must be a detailed brief before the work starts. That way everyone can see the scope of the work and can assess how much he is going to be asked to do himself. Writing yourself a set of objectives (see pages 98–102) is the most unambiguous way to approach the brief and will be one of the best ways of ensuring that the project is a successful and fulfilling exercise for everyone involved.

Checklist on projects

Are you clear about the educational objectives of the project? ☐

Are they relevant and worthwhile? ☐

Could you defend it honestly and vigorously against anyone who accused you of 'getting research done on the cheap'? ☐

Does the project draw on many academic disciplines? ☐

Have you obtained adequate resources to run the project? ☐

Is it obvious that the tasks are fairly distributed? ☐

Are existing skills in the group being used? ☐

Have you planned to help people acquire the technical skills they will need to do the research? ☐

Do the tasks give everyone in the group the opportunities for serious learning? ☐

Have you planned how the project results will be publicized? ☐

12

Discussion

In the quotes below all the tutors and students quoted felt sure that 'discussion' accurately described what was going on in their groups:

> After an hour-and-a-quarter lecture from me we have a coffee break, then discussion. The class usually raises such pertinent points that lengthy answers are needed from me, so that it sometimes needs miniature lectures to give a satisfactory reply. The class is exhausting for this reason.

> During discussion we are speaking to each other, exploring, exchanging views, learning from each other: tutor from student, students from tutor, students from students.

> I dislike the discussion part of the class because some members (not me) always lose their tempers.

> He is a very good teacher and we have a lot of interesting discussions, but he does love us to come round to his point of view!

> In discussion I believe in quick-fire, question-and-answer technique. It keeps them on their toes.

> I encourage them to be frank. The content of the course (psychology) is less important than the business of learning to work as a group and getting to know yourself. I say virtually nothing. They do all the talking.

Clearly, there are wide variations in the activities of these classes. One tutor seems to talk all the time, another says 'virtually nothing'; the atmosphere of the discussion in one class is mild and conversational, in another it is fierce and argumentative, in yet another personal and intense. Most important of all, all the quotes show something of the fundamental divergences of opinion about the purpose and value of the discussion process itself, a divergence often concealed by the umbrella of a word such as 'discussion' which has such vague and uncomfortable associations.

Some tutors clearly believe that the point of a discussion is to change the attitudes of the class, usually in the direction of the tutor's views on a particular issue. Others believe in discussion because students enjoy it and they think there should be parts of a class which students enjoy. Others again are never quite sure why they do it, but feel that somehow it must be a good thing. With this theoretical vagueness 'discussion', as it is usually applied, can mean anything from a few questions tossed to a class at the end of a gruelling lecture session to a solemn ninety minutes given over entirely to something very near group therapy.

What is 'discussion'?

Group therapy has its value, so does a question-and-answer session, so does a debate, but none of these processes is authentic discussion. A rough definition of real, as opposed to imitation, discussion might be that it is a situation where students and tutor can and do make an open, equal and personal response to a book, a philosophical theory, an industrial-relations problem, a current fashion in dress, a social trend, or anything else which needs interpretation to take it beyond a factual statement. The implications of this sort of discussion are that in controversial personal, social and academic areas, students, as adult members of society, have as much right to articulate and expect respect for their points of view as do tutors.

Discussion defined in this way is a very different thing from what passes for discussion in many adult classes. It becomes a time when tutors show their classes that they have abandoned their teaching roles as such, that they are encouraging what R. W. K. Paterson describes as a 'common search for meanings. For two people to "discuss" some piece of news is for them to ask each other "What does it mean?"'*

This search for meanings is frequently given the educational

* R. W. K. Paterson, 'The concept of discussion', *Studies in Adult Education*, vol. 2, no. 1, 1970.

justification that it consolidates knowledge, improves the social atmosphere of the group, allows people to test themselves, and so on, but in fact discussion is in itself a supremely valuable process, whether it is used for a few minutes in a computing class or whether it becomes the main method of learning in a sociology group. To quote Paterson again:

> To unfold the meaning of a poem by discovering oneself and one's world in face of the poem, to experience the sympathetic, critical, understanding, puzzled, consenting, or demurring responses of others similarly occupied, and to respond in turn to their self-disclosures and self-commitments – to do all this is surely to engage in a type of activity which is educationally ultimate.

Tutors and authority

Many tutors would claim that they already have the sort of respect for their students which makes the discussions in their classrooms as free as it is possible to make them. However, we can too easily assume the tremendous mantle of authority the profession has acquired from teaching children. Furthermore, many of us are unaware of how much influence we have with our classes and of how easily this influence can be exerted affectionately as well as brusquely. It is often as easy for the teacher of adults to do this as it is for the schoolteacher, given the diffidence of an inexperienced adult student, or of a new class of students anxious not to declare themselves too soon:

> I thought I'd let other people do all the talking. I felt too ignorant to open my mouth.

> I knew I'd blush if I spoke, so I never spoke.

> Discussion is all right for those who are well informed. Other people always seem to know so much more than me.

Classroom discussions, closely analysed, will often reveal how frequently tutors capitalize on their traditional authority and on the humble feelings of their students. As a result, many discussions in adult education and training, are far from free or equal, because tutors, often quite unconsciously, guide, manipulate and dominate proceedings. For instance, you may feel obliged to follow every comment from a student with a longer one of your own. Students will hardly ever talk to other students under this system, the communication may be brisk and lively, but it will be in several sets of two-way traffic, student to tutor, tutor to student. An analysis of this sort of discussion usually reveals that the tutor talks almost all the time.

It is hard discipline as a tutor to keep your mouth shut, to listen, and to show signs of listening instead of talking. Most tutors are good at talking and especially enjoy talking about their subject. Not talking can be exquisite agony, as any experienced tutor will know.

Some tutors may encourage student contributions, but may set up what has accurately been diagnosed as a 'guessing-game'. The game is played so that the student can hardly ever win, as in this brief transcript from a class comparing two poems by Wordsworth. The atmosphere of the class was entirely friendly and informal.

Tutor: Well now, you've read the second poem again, I hope. (*Murmurs of agreement.*) One thing that struck me, one thing I'm wondering, did you see any striking difference between this poem and the last one we read?

Student 1: It's longer! (*Laughter and pause.*)

Tutor: Well . . . yes!

Student 2: It is that this poem is somehow more . . . well, not so personal, it seems to have less of Wordsworth himself in it?

Tutor: Yes. But I was thinking of something else.

Student 3: The language is not so rich? Fewer metaphors?

Tutor: Yes, a good point. That's certainly true. We'll look at that later. Anyone got any more ideas?

Student 1: I don't like it! (*Laughter.*)

Tutor: Any more bright ideas? (*Pause.*) Well, what I was thinking was that this poem is much more in the ballad vein, isn't it? It's reminiscent of the old simple Scottish ballads – can anyone tell us what a ballad is?

The tutor's views

In this situation the teacher has said in effect to the class, 'Now guess what I've got in mind?' The trouble is that there may be dozens of legitimate points of comparison between two poems, any one of which he may have in mind. The class plays along for a while, then says or signifies by silence the equivalent of 'I give up', after which the tutor announces the 'answer'. Not only does this sort of technique suggest to a class that there is only one acceptable and right major point of comparison, it also suggests that responses to a poem have to be tackled in a particular order (the suggestion about metaphor was pushed aside for 'later'), and that it is the response the tutor himself has in mind which is the most important one. Such discussion technique ignores the possibility that students themselves can and should make fresh and direct contributions of a quality which would surprise tutors who think theirs are the only interpretations which count.

Guessing-games develop out of a confusion between 'real' discussion and 'question and answer'. There are subjects – mathematics, for instance – where it might be legitimate for a tutor to say something like 'Can anyone tell me what the square root of forty-four is?' because there is only one possible answer. It is surprising how few such subjects are, and at what a low factual and academic level they have to function for it to be possible to deal with them in so summary a fashion.

Tutors may press their own views in other, more subtle ways. They may reward someone who offers a view agreeing with their own by nodding vigorously or by saying, 'Yes, a good point', or by following it up with some forceful elaboration of their own. They may frown doubtfully at a student giving an opposite opinion, or simply by the coolness of their nod on receiving the comment imply that only courtesy prevents them saying that such a comment was ridiculous, or inappropriate. They may initiate the discussion and prod it along with leading questions, as in this sociology class (again the atmosphere of this particular class was noticeably relaxed and uninhibited):

Tutor: Don't you think society is still rather hard on unmarried mums?

Student 1: Well, no, it's much easier now for a girl to keep her baby, isn't it?

Tutor: But don't we all disapprove secretly of someone breaking the code?

Student 2: The girl gets all the blame.

Student 3: It's the child that suffers.

Student 4: There's a girl living near us with a baby and people avoid her. I think they feel embarrassed by her.
Tutor: Do you talk to her?
Student 4: Well – now and again, but I don't know her very well. She keeps herself to herself.
Tutor: Why do you think this is? Is it because society punishes deviants? Isn't it that we all feel threatened by someone who has chosen not to conform?
Student 2: Yes.
Student 3: That's true.

The phrasing of the tutor's initial question has given the class a clue either to his own view, or to what he interprets as the common view of a familiar social problem. It may be that the tutor can offer the class evidence on how 'society' views single, unmarried mothers – surveys, novels, articles – but he notably does not do this. He quickly tries to encourage the group to confess to prejudice themselves, and seizes on a personal anecdote told by one student as the occasion to drive home his point by virtually accusing the student who told it of prejudice herself. In such discussion the tutor gives it a gloss of freedom, but in fact he is seeking confirmation of his own view and moral standpoint (and in the extract quoted, eventually wins it superficially) almost as firmly as the tutor in the guessing-game.

The information and sources that tutors use for discussion may easily be chosen to support their own views. The group here is usually at the mercy of the teacher unless its members are lucky enough or enterprising enough to discover the bias for themselves:

> Between school and university I took a year's voluntary job, but to keep my hand in I thought I'd go to an extra-mural class in my own subject – history. It appealed to me because it was advertised as a course using original documents of the period, with lots of opportunities for discussion. It was very interesting and the lecturer was superb – a real enthusiast. I only discovered how incredibly partisan his view of the period was when in my third year at university I realized how his enthusiasm for one school of thought had totally affected the documents he gave us and the evidence we used for our discussions. He was quite unaware of what he had done, I'm sure.

The dangers of planning

Some tutors attempt to control a discussion by drawing up detailed plans for it in advance. Control can become manipulation where a tutor also tries to anticipate the content of the students' answers. It is fair enough to have a rough plan in mind and to have at hand the materials and information needed to explore the likely ramifications of the three or four questions any one class could be expected to explore in a few hours, but you should always be prepared to abandon this plan if the interest of the class points clearly in another direction. What seems a red herring to you may well be an absorbing topic to your students. Each red herring should be judged on its merits by the group as well as by you. It certainly seems a mistake to have too many rigid expectations about the length, content and likely conclusions of a discussion. In opening up discussion you are offering the class something free, floating and unpredictable. It is not possible to chart too closely in advance the form the discussion should take, for the essence of a valuable discussion is the unexpectedness and originality of the new territory which should constantly be explored. It is only when your students can see that you are genuinely offering them opportunities to speculate, think and interpret that new ideas will flourish.

A good discussion inevitably exposes the ambiguities and complexities of a topic. Many tutors, searching for a way to find a framework for their students that will hold widely diverging views, will attempt to impose a 'conclusion' on the discussion which can easily be a false representation of what has been said:

> It puzzled me at first, but I never recognized his summaries as accounts of what we had all said. After a bit I realized that the summary represented (a) his own opinion, (b) what he wished we had said. I think we must have disappointed him by not being such a bright class as he'd hoped. We certainly weren't up to his standards.

Paterson makes the same point from an educationist's view:

> One inevitably wonders how many . . . counterfeit discussions are staged in adult classes by tutors whose confidence in their own preferred views disables them from taking the views of their students with the utmost seriousness required of all the participants in authentic educational dialogue. I am referring

> less to the assertive and dogmatic tutor than to the kind of tutor who unobtrusively and skilfully synthesises the various discussion contributions of his students, by judicious selection and emphasis, into a neatly structured and rounded proposition or body of propositions, which are then represented as the 'conclusions' of the 'class discussion' although they have in fact been evolved by the tutor, who has ingeniously utilised the discussion, always more or less under his discreet control, as an educational device for arraying precisely this body of propositions, deemed by him to be of some importance to his students at this stage of their classwork. The teaching skill exercised by such a tutor may be of a very high order, and the results gained may be of great educational value. To the extent that his students believe themselves to be participating in a genuinely open-ended dialogue, however, they are being misled; and to the extent that he believes himself to be 'conducting a discussion', he is misleading himself.*

It is, of course, your job to present a discussion to a group in such a way that members can see they have learnt from it, but it seems a false way to set about this delicate task by using phrases such as 'Well, I think we're all agreed that . . .' or 'Everyone seems to have come to the conclusion that . . .'. It is highly unlikely that all students are of one mind on any topic worth extended discussion, and it is your task to see that a false consensus does not emerge. You should encourage and maintain divergent views, even where they conflict sharply with your own. As Albert Mansbridge said: 'The class is not intended for the passing or resolutions, but is rather a means whereby all relevant facts and arguments may be looked at and turned over'.

Controversial issues

However, it is easier to look at and turn over some facts than others. On many of the issues which come up in adult classes, tutors as well as students may have such strong opinions that they find it hard to resist voicing them. Making an outburst is one thing, using your authority to deliver some final *coup de grâce* on the argument is

* Paterson, 'The concept of discussion', *Studies in Adult Education*, vol. 2, no. 1, 1970.

another. If you are too cool you will be resented by your classes; if you are too heated you may lose their respect:

> I remember one discussion on race – a topic chosen by the group (young adults) where I sat back and let them get on with it. This was in Birmingham and there was a fair sprinkling of black students in the group. I was frankly appalled by the massive generalisations and contradictory assertions voiced by those who should have known better. All those terrible statements like – 'They take all the jobs' but 'live on national assistance'. Those hoary old apocryphal stories were trotted out – 'I know a man who lives next door to them – and they pee in the back garden.' All that sort of thing. Perhaps what annoyed me most was their attitude towards the black students there, they were so insensitive even when one – a popular black student – got up and left, obviously very upset.
>
> Just before the end of the session I decided I could contain myself no longer and took charge. I rounded on them and told them if I were black I would feel like those in the Black Power movement – I would scream 'Burn, baby, burn' – I would feel my only hope was to destroy by physical means the white man's domination.
>
> I am afraid they were horribly shocked by my outburst. It took a lot of time before our relationship returned to normal.

How can you avoid uncomfortable situations like this? How do you recognize and cope with your own bias but still use the discussion method? How can information and ideas of all sorts be presented to the group so that both discussion and learning take place?

One possible solution was developed by the Humanities Project of the Schools Council. It was aimed at adolescents but had useful implications for adult education, too. The project investigated ways of dealing with controversial topics through discussion rather than instruction, and defined a controversial issue as

> one which divides students, parents and teachers because it involves an element of value judgement which prevents the issue being settled by evidence and experiment.
>
> There may be consensus among students, parents and teachers at high levels of generality, an agreement, for example,

> that other things being equal, war is a bad thing. In practice this does not help the teacher, since effective discussion concentrates for much of the time on specific issues which are inevitably highly controversial.*

Laurence Stenhouse, the Project Director, came to the conclusion that the only tenable position for a teacher wishing to introduce such important and controversial topics in a classroom is to adopt a 'value-neutral' position. The 'value-neutral' teacher is aware of his own bias, but 'as students often put it, the teacher may agree not to take sides in their discussion'. Since the teacher who adopts this stance can no longer be the sole source of information, the project developed and published a battery of 'evidence' – by which it means any relevant poetry, drama, photographs, tapes, films – around major themes, such as War or the Family, which become the centre of a discussion in which the teacher acts as procedural guide but not moral mentor.

The Project itself was too radical for many schools. The methods it advocated involved profound changes in the teacher's role, and seemed to many teachers to rob them of prized chances to give advice to vulnerable adolescents. Management of the plethora of resources was tricky both from a logistic and a moral point of view, since the teacher might continue to push his own opinion through the 'evidence' he offered the group. Management of the students proved exhausting, the authority of the teacher, and his relationships within the class and the school, changed drastically towards a more democratic and egalitarian situation to which many teachers found it hard to adjust.

Nevertheless, the teaching strategy was shown to work, and its principles have been applied as successfully in adult education, where there is a healthy tradition of discussion in classes and where the procedures of the project have been valuably extended to more factual subjects.

Investment of emotion

Emotion comes even into judging facts and superficially more neutral scientific subjects, as was interestingly shown by M. L.

* Humanities Curriculum Project, *The Humanities Project: An Introduction*, Schools Council and Nuffield Foundation, Heinemann, 1970.

Johnson Abercrombie in a classic experiment with medical students who, in one set of 'free' discussions (that is, with no academic direction from a teacher), were asked to compare two radiographs of a hand. The results showed how many unjustifiable assertions the students were inclined to make on sparse evidence, how frequently they saw what they expected to see, and how emotionally they would defend their conclusions:

> The inferences the students had made were not arrived at as a result of a series of logical steps, but swiftly, almost unconsciously. The validity of the inferences was usually not inquired into, indeed the process was usually accompanied by a feeling of certainty of being right, and consequently the discussion of incompatible views sometimes became very heated. Frequently the correct inference had been made (as with the statement that A was a younger hand than B), and then discussion did not change the formulation of the end results, but only brought to light the processes involved in getting it.*

This concern with evidence, with logical processes, with the distinction between factual information and what can be deduced from it, is the educational end which discussion is superbly well equipped to fulfil. Abercrombie summarizes her aim in the course of unguided discussions as being

> to make it possible for the student to relinquish the security of thinking in well-defined given channels and to find a new kind of stability based on the recognition and acceptance of ambiguity, uncertainty and open choice.

This might well serve as an aim for most of the courses in adult education which use a discussion method as one of their tools.

The flow of resources

'Free' group discussion is sometimes denigrated as 'the pooling of ignorance', and, clearly, if discussion is to be more than this, the group must have a constant flow of new information and ideas. Traditionally these have come from the tutor, but you are as a tutor

* M. L. Johnson Abercrombie, *The Anatomy of Judgement*, Hutchinson, 1960; Penguin, 1969.

at the mercy of your own bias, probably as much in academic subjects as in matters of value judgement. In a course where there is no lecturing at all from the tutor and where the learning is done entirely through discussion, then your role becomes more concentrated on the flow of resources, many of which might be digested outside the class time: for instance, videos, novels, audio tapes or open learning texts. If you do not have the benefit of a ready-made 'multi-media' course you can still construct one – with the expense of more time, trouble and cost, of course – by establishing your own collection of documents, tapes and photographs, to which you and your group can constantly add. All discussion is demanding, but the more nearly it approaches an open exchange of views of the Humanities Project type, the greater the skill it will demand of you.

Problems

Free discussion may solve some problems, but it undoubtedly creates others. For instance, some students are satisfied enough with a tutor who is willing to tell them what to think, and may be quite happy with the appearance and not the substance of discussion, simply because a substantial discussion in an educational setting may be unfamiliar as well as demanding. The only school experience of 'discussion' many people have may well be something close in spirit to the dismal process Charles Dickens satirized in *Hard Times* over a hundred years ago, when he set the first scene of his attack on the cold spirit of utilitarianism in Mr Gradgrind's school during a visit by a 'government officer' – perhaps an earlier, grimmer version of a modern HMI:

> 'Bitzer', said Thomas Gradgrind. 'Your definition of a horse.'
>
> 'Quadruped. Graminivorous. Forty teeth, namely twenty-four grinders, four eye-teeth, and twelve incisive. Sheds coat in the spring; in marshy countries, sheds hoofs, too. Hoofs hard, but requiring to be shod with iron. Age known by marks in mouth.' Thus (and much more) Bitzer.
>
> 'Now girl number twenty,' said Mr Gradgrind. 'You know what a horse is.'
>
> She curtseyed again, and would have blushed deeper, if she could have blushed deeper than she had blushed all this time.

Bitzer, after rapidly blinking at Thomas Gradgrind with both eyes at once, and so catching the light upon his quivering ends of lashes that they looked like the antennae of busy insects, put his knuckles to his freckled forehead and sat down again.

The third gentleman now stepped forth. A mighty man at cutting and drying, he was; a government officer; in his way (and in most other people's too), a professed pugilist; always in training, always with a system to force down the general throat like a bolus, always to be heard of at the bar of his little Public-office, ready to fight All England. To continue in fistic phraseology, he had a genius for coming up to the scratch, wherever and whatever it was, and proving himself an ugly customer. He would go in and damage any subject whatever with his right, follow up with his left, stop, exchange, counter, bore his opponent (he always fought All England) to the ropes, and fall upon him neatly. He was certain to knock the wind out of common-sense, and render that unlucky adversary deaf to the call of time. And he had it in charge from high authority to bring about the great public-office Millennium, when Commissioners should reign upon earth.

'Very well,' said this gentleman, briskly smiling, and folding his arms. 'That's a horse. Now, let me ask you girls and boys, Would you paper a room with representations of horses?'

After a pause, one half of the children cried in chorus, 'Yes, sir!' Upon which the other half, seeing in the gentleman's face that 'Yes' was wrong, cried out in chorus, 'No, sir!' – as the custom is, in these examinations.

'Of course, No. Why wouldn't you?'

A pause. One corpulent slow boy, with a wheezy manner of breathing, ventured the answer. Because he wouldn't paper a room at all, but would paint it.

'You *must* paper it,' said Thomas Gradgrind, 'whether you like it or not. Don't tell *us* you wouldn't paper it. What do you mean, boy?'

'I'll explain to you, then,' said the gentleman, after another and a dismal pause, 'why you wouldn't paper a room with representations of horses. Do you ever see horses walking up and down the sides of rooms in reality – in fact? Do you?'

'Yes, sir!' from one half. 'No, sir!' from the other.

'Of course no,' said the gentleman, with an indignant look at

> the wrong half. 'Why, then you are not to see anywhere, what you don't see in fact; you are not to have anywhere, what you don't have in fact. What is called Taste, is only another name for Fact.'

Students accustomed to a tutor who seems omniscient may take time to find the courage to speak freely in a class, or to believe that their contributions really are being taken seriously. Indeed, after a while, when it is clear that they are being listened to with scrupulous attention by tutor and other students, this may in itself be alarming. A student who can throw in a frivolous comment in a discussion dominated by the tutor may be overwhelmed by the responsibility of speaking in a serious discussion where the emphasis is on the students.

Others may resent it if you do not take a dominant role, and may attack you by saying something like 'You're the teacher, you've studied the subject longer than we have. Why don't you tell us?' This situation sometimes develops in a class where the tutor is clearly keeping something up her sleeve, and deceiving the class about her own opinion or holding back useful knowledge. I once watched a tutor, who believed in never under any circumstances giving his own view, attacked by an exasperated class after he had answered perhaps the tenth direct question from one of his students with 'I don't know, what do you think?' He received the tart and well-deserved response 'But you do know and you ought to tell us.'

Discussion can often seem ragged and inconclusive, especially to students used to learning one 'right' answer. These students may find the ambiguity of a discussion too trying, and many others will feel that 'just talking' is a waste of time. These students might share Professor Max Beloff's view that 'the don teaches the boy: he knows more', a view that denies the possibility that students can and frequently do surpass the master and learn from each other, especially when opportunities are made for them to do so, and when the skills of discussion are learnt by students as well as practised by the tutor. Nevertheless, many discussions can seem time-wasting, and with adult classes relying heavily on the discussion process you will find it essential to try various ways of consolidating the discussion. The possibilities will include notetaking, written work based on the discussion, or personal research undertaken as a result of points made during it, as well as progress reports, or discussions on the discussions.

This kind of work can also be the occasion for correcting the mistakes and factual errors inevitably made by students in the course of discussion. Mistakes you diagnose as 'dangerous' can properly be corrected in the classroom, but the responsibility for doing this need not always be yours. Usually there are plenty of students as capable of making the correction. Otherwise, a quiet word after the class or before the next one is usually more effective than a public reproof.

Conflict and argument

You are ultimately responsible for the mood and atmosphere of your class. Hectic, fevered discussion can arouse a priceless interest and excitement in a topic, and it does no harm to bring disputes into the open. Sometimes, however, discussions become so heated and the participants so involved that they become angry. Discussion can then be confused with argument, with one 'side' of a class ranged implacably against the other. The point of the discussion turns away from the educational objective of exchanging opinions, listening to and learning from other people, and turns instead into a battle where one side has to concede defeat and lose face:

> Every time the class met, although it was nineteenth-century social and political history we were discussing, the discussion always got round to politics today. We all knew Mr ____ was a keen Labour man because he was on the Council. He didn't say it himself, but I felt he used to encourage one or two others to argue it out. Sometimes it got nasty and there would be name-calling, etc. On one occasion it was serious and one of his opponents was so angry he refused to come to the pub afterwards. I felt the teacher ought to have stopped it but it was hard to see what more she could have done other than try to keep the peace a bit better.

In a situation like this 'education' has gone. People who are encouraged to state extreme views with such vigour are well on the way to finding it impossible to listen to anyone else. Having committed themselves vehemently and publicly to one view, it becomes difficult to retract or to explore the possibility that other people may have a view which is equally valid. The point of discussion should not be to establish a majority view, or even any one range of views, but to develop understanding, to learn how to make up one's mind, how to assess evidence, how to formulate conclusions. The conclusion itself may well be an irrelevance. When you see argument rather than discussion developing you will do well to use your authority to cool the atmosphere with a joke or an invitation to examine some evidence, or to ask some other students to contribute.

It may be that some tutors are glad to see arguments develop because tutors tend to evaluate the discussions in their classrooms in terms of how 'stimulating' or 'lively' they are. Not all discussions need to be noisy or obviously vigorous to be educationally valuable. A good discussion may be quiet, apparently low-key, with a lot of thoughtful silences. Some tutors are afraid of silence and leap in to fill any pause that looks like becoming an embarrassment, perhaps because long silences have connections with social embarrassment. A class which has established that a pause can continue until someone is ready to fill it with a considered comment may well produce more measured and telling points than the hastier, superficial sparkle of a lively, non-stop discussion.

Individual contributions

Nevertheless, in a good discussion most members of a group feel willing and able to speak when appropriate. Many of the anxieties of tutors and the grumbles of students concern the numbers of people participating in any one discussion. Three typical comments illustrate familiar situations:

> A lot of people there had been going to these classes for years. They knew each other and they knew the tutor, so no one else got a look in.

> My *bête-noire* was a man who would always try to prove me wrong at great length. He was being forced by his union to attend, so he always felt he had to show he already knew everything that I was teaching. He tried to dominate every discussion.

> I always thought our discussions were good, but one evening for interest, I counted up the number who had said something. I was horrified to discover that only six out of sixteen had said anything.

Even in a group where everybody contributes at some time, there will be always be some who talk more than others. This can be a cause for concern if those who talk most are preventing other people from joining in, or are seeming to waste the group's time with rambling anecdotes, with harangues, or simply with information too difficult for the rest of the group to understand. Adult groups often contain one member who is more knowledgeable than the rest. You may find it tempting to engage one prominent student in discussion – sometimes simply out of pleasure in talking, sometimes because of a cowardly wish to placate a student who might otherwise become bored and restless. The short-term solution is to let him get on with it, but if you habitually allow one student to dominate a class you are only storing up trouble for the future. It is unfair to other students, who eventually become irritated and fidgety and may leave the class rather than sit through more sessions of a dialogue between a teacher and an apparently favoured student.

It is better instead to encourage students to develop self-criticism about the quality and length of their own contributions. You can set the pace by inviting the group to evaluate each other's contributions: 'Does any one have a comment of that?' or 'What do other people think?' In a class where this capacity has been encouraged, students are often able to interrupt a lengthy contribution either with challenges and questions, with comments of their own or, as I saw once in a philosophy class, simply with a good-humoured, 'You've had three minutes by my watch, time to let someone else in now!'

Nevertheless, dominant members of groups are often able and energetic people, whose initiative and enthusiasm can be valuable to the rest of the group, either in the ideas they contribute to general discussion, or in the extra research, short lectures and special assignments they may occasionally be encouraged to undertake. It is sometimes hard to keep a careful balance between letting them tyrannize a group, on the one hand, and letting them waste their talents, on the other. You may find that you can speak privately to an over-talkative student, asking him or her to talk less. This can sometimes be effective and may be the appropriate thing to do, but you run the risk of seeming impertinent or else suggesting a conspiracy between yourself and your specially clever student, with both of you agreeing to patronize the less fortunate slower people.

Silent members of a class, or people who speak only rarely in a discussion, can present problems when you do not want to bully people into speaking but also want to see everyone make some sort of contribution. People who do not speak can be silent as a way of showing disapproval of what the rest of the group are saying; they can be silent out of shyness or diffidence or laziness; silent because although they would like to speak, conditions never seem right for them to take the plunge; or simply silent because they prefer to listen to other people rather than to talk themselves.

You must judge each case on its merits. There is no evidence to equate participation in discussion with learning, and if people prefer to be silent it could be an impertinence to try forcing them to speak. Attempting to draw out a shy student by asking direct questions may face him or her with an excruciating ordeal and may, in any case, fail to produce a response. I remember a student in one of my classes who simply stonewalled this attempt to be helpful by shaking her head silently and staring down at the desk. Other students may feel you have provided them with just the opening they have been waiting for, but your effort will usually be more successful if directed more widely than at a single individual – 'Some of you have special knowledge of ____. Would any of you like to say something on this?' Again, the rest of the group can be encouraged to look to each other for contributions, to get to know who has particular knowledge of or unusual opinions on some issue and can therefore be expected to say something valuable.

When a shy or less dominant member does make a brief contribution to a discussion, it is often helpful to rein in the discussion at that point to ask the student for further elaboration – 'It might be interesting if you expanded that point'. Alternatively, you can suggest a general pause in the discussion by saying something like, 'We seem to have covered a lot of ground rather quickly. Can we stop to think for a moment?' Focusing the discussion at one stage like this is often a useful way of allowing slower thinkers to catch up and speak if they want to. There may be opportunities to do the same thing at the beginning and end of a discussion. I have seen some tutors encourage silent students to speak at these points by saying, 'We left a lot unsaid at our last session. Is there anyone who would like the last word?' Such invitations have, of course, to be followed by a generous pause otherwise they might just as well not be made.

Problems of over-dominant and too silent members can often be solved by splitting the group into smaller groups for some part of the class time:

> We start off as one group – about fifteen of us – going over the week's written work, looking at a new poem or chapter. After coffee we divide into however many groups can be divided by three or four. Each group has a question written on a piece of paper. All the questions are closely related but different, and based on the topic we discussed before coffee. This takes twenty minutes, strictly timed. We then report back, compare questions, and have what is usually a most useful general discussion to finish off. With this system everybody who wants to can speak, and everyone is obliged to give really close attention to the text.

> There are twenty-five students, two tutors. We watch the video together, discuss it for ten minutes, then split. People who never speak in the large group normally say quite a lot in the smaller one.

It is not unusual for the first five minutes of the discussion to be the slowest and the most difficult to manage, and the part of the process that you may dread most. The best ways of encouraging discussion seem to be to ask students to prepare for it by thinking, reading and writing, to reassure them that silence does not matter, to make it clear that you really have withdrawn from your role of pedagogue by saying 'Would anyone like to comment?' or some such phrase and no more. Most importantly, you must provide the group with an initial stimulus as emotionally gripping, or as intellectually intriguing and as complex, as possible. This could be a lecture, a dramatic reading, a film, a case study or simulation or anything else which demands an immediate response. Film and video are perhaps particularly useful in loosening tongues, as many people are used to discussing them informally without the strain that may be associated with academic discussion of a poem or book.

Remember, too, how much the shape of the room and the type of furniture (see page 83) contribute to atmosphere and eyelines. If your aim is a discussion which involves everyone, it is more or less essential to seat the group in comfortable chairs ranged in a circle, as that is the only way people can see or address each other easily. Where you have a group sitting lecture-style in straight lines, most people will only have one good view, and that is of you, so naturally they will be far more likely to address their remarks to you than to each other. The temptation to cap every student comment with one of your own will be almost irresistible.

The tutor's role in discussion

Your role in an authentic discussion is, then, a taxing one. You must first of all make sure that the students understand and share a common view of what discussion is by inviting them at the outset to discuss the discussion process, and by making it clear that your own role will be that of impartial chairman rather than active teacher, of careful listener rather than frequent speaker. You must be ready to clarify issues so that groups understand what they are discussing, and why. You must be ready to relate the issues of one discussion to issues raised and explored on previous occasions. You must see that the group eschews personal attacks and violent sarcasm, as well as dull statement of old prejudices. You must encourage and protect minority views. You should make sure that students learn to distinguish between fact and opinion, and be ready to feed in the resources which could supply facts and opinions giving an opposite, even an unpopular view. You must set the linguistic tone by using language everyone can understand. You must make sure that opportunities are kept open so that people who want to speak can speak. You must encourage the art of listening as well as talking.

If you can do all this, and at the same time train your group to take over these functions, too, you are offering your class a chance to learn in a unique way, by measuring minds and experiences with other people on equal terms.

The philosophical and democratic case for discussion, as well as by implication its educational justification, has never been made so powerfully as by John Stuart Mill in *On Liberty*, a case which can still serve as a model to any adult tutor today:

> There must be discussion, to show how experience is to be interpreted. Wrong opinions and practices gradually yield to fact and argument; but facts and arguments, to produce any effect on the mind, must be brought before it. Very few facts are able to tell their own story, without comments to bring out their meaning. The whole strength and value, then, of human judgement, depending on the one property, that it can be set

> right when it is wrong, is that reliance can be placed on it only when the means of setting it right are kept constantly at hand. In the case of any person whose judgement is really deserving of confidence, how has it become so? Because he has kept his mind open to criticism of his opinions and conduct. Because it has been his practice to listen to all that could be said against him; to profit by as much of it as was just, and expound to himself, and upon occasion to others, the fallacy of what was fallacious. Because he has felt that the only way in which a human being can make some approach to knowing the whole of a subject, is by hearing what can be said about it by persons of every variety of opinion, and studying all modes in which it can be looked at by every character of mind. No wise man ever acquired his wisdom in any mode but this; nor is it in the nature of human intellect to become wise in any other manner.

Checklist on discussion

Are you clear in your own mind about the distinctions between question-and-answer and discussion? ☐

Have you provided enough resources for all members of the group to be able to contribute an opinion if they want to? ☐

Does the group understand the 'rules' of discussion? ☐

Do you avoid imposing false 'conclusions' at the end of a discussion? ☐

On the other hand, do you provide summaries of evidence – either in writing or verbally? ☐

Are you and your group able to tolerate pauses and silences? ☐

Do the individuals in the group participate equally, or are there some who are over-dominant? ☐

Do you use effective techniques for persuading quieter people to participate if they want to? ☐

Bibliography

Abercrombie, M. L. Johnson, *The Anatomy of Judgement*. Penguin, 2nd edn, 1969.

Beard, R., *Teaching and Learning in Higher Education*. Penguin, 3rd edn, 1976.

Belbin, E. and Belbin, R. M., *Problems in Adult Retraining*. Heineman, 1972.

Bligh, D. A., 'What's the Use of Lectures?', D. A. and B. Bligh, Briar House, Exeter.

Bloom, B. (ed.), *Taxonomy of Educational Objectives – Book I, The Cognitive Domain*. Longman, 1956.

Bruner, J. S., *Towards a Theory of Instruction*. W. W. Norton and Co., New York, 1968.

Buzan, T., *Use your Head*, BBC, 2nd edn, 1986.

Coates, K. and Silburn, R., 'St Ann's: poverty, deprivation and morale in a Nottingham community'. Department of Adult Education, University of Nottingham, 1967.

Gagné, R. M., *The Conditions of Learning*. Holt, Rinehart and Winston, New York, 3rd edn, 1977.

Gibbs, G., *Teaching Students to Learn*. Open University Press, 1981.

Houle, C. O., *The Inquiring Mind*. University of Wisconsin Press, Madison, 1961.

Hutchinson, E. and Hutchinson, E. M., *Learning Later*. Routledge and Kegan Paul, 1978.

Jarvis, P., *Adult and Continuing Education: Theory and Practice*. Croom Helm, 1983.

Johnstone, J. W. C. and Rivera, R. J., *Volunteers for Learning*. Aldine, Chicago, 1965.

Klein, J., *Working with Groups*. Hutchinson, 2nd edn, 1965.

Knowles, M. S., *The Adult Learner, A Neglected Species*. Gulf Publishing Co., Houston, 1978.

Rogers, A., *Teaching Adults*. Open University Press, 1986.

Rogers, C., Encounter Groups. Allen Lane, 1970.

Rogers, J. (ed.), *Adults in Education*, BBC, 3rd edn, 1984.

Rogers, J. and Groombridge, B., *Right to Learn*. Arrow, 1976.
Thompson, J. L. (ed.), *Adult Education for a Change*. Heinemann, 1980.
Thorndike, E. C., *Adult Learning*, Macmillan, 1928.
Tight, M., *Education for Adults, Vol 1: Adult Learning and Education*. Croom Helm, 1983.
Tough, A. *The Adult's Learning Project*. Ontario Institute for Studies in Education, Toronto, 3rd edn, 1981.

Index

Abercrombie, M.L.J., 184
absenteeism, 36
ACCA, 30, 144
accountancy-entrants, 7
activity, in learning, 40–3, 47
Adult Literacy Campaign, 32
adult non-readers, 14, 32
ageing, 15–19
Alcoholics Anonymous, 74
anxiety
  in learners, 9–26, 136, 146, 147
  in tutors, 69
argument, in classes, 77, 188, 189
arousal, necessary for adult learners, 54
assessment, 152
attitude changing, 133
authoritarian leadership style, 72, 73

background information on learners, 95
Barratt-Brown, M., 46
BBC, 3, 4, 50, 64, 149
Belbin, E. and Belbin, M., 42, 43, 59
Beloff, M., 187
British Rail, driver training, 42, 43
broadcasting, 5, 148, 149

Carlyle, T., 124
cardiopulmonary resuscitation (CPR), 51
case study method, 126–42
Cash, T., 4
Coates, K., 159, 164, 165
competencies, 100
competition, 74
conflict, 77, 78, 188
Cooper Marsh, I., 70, 71
correspondence tuition, 8, 143

democratic leadership style, 72, 73
demonstration method, 118–25
Department of Education and Science (DES), 6
Dickens, C., 185–7
discipline, challenges to, 36
discovery method, 43
discussion method, 119, 174–94
distance learning, *see* open learning
Dunning, J., 163

Employment Training, 33
enrolment, 94, 95
essays, 55, 162
expectancy theory, 36
experience in learners, 52, 53

feedback on learning, 57–68, 120, 151
  in open learning, 154–7

flexibility, 47
flexistudy, 8
first session of class, 105–17
furniture, *see* room arrangement

games, academic, *see* case study
GCSE, 29, 32, 35
Government training schemes, 29
groups, management, 69–90
'guessing games' in discussion, 177–9

handouts, 122
Hawking, S., 80
Hertzberg, F., 35
Hoggart, R., 81
Humanities Project, 182, 183
Hunt, A., 170
'hygeine' factors, 35

'icebreakers', 111
Institute of Personnel Management (IPM), 30
institutional
  pressure, 86
  inefficiency, 93

Job Training Scheme, 32

'laissez-faire' leaders, 72,
lateness in learners, 36, 37, 115
Leach, E., 17, 18
learner anxieties, *see* anxiety in learners
learner
  expectations, 22–5
  experience, 52–4
  pressure on tutors, 87
  reasons for leaving, *see* motivation
  social class, 19, 20, 21
learning to learn, 55
Leavis, F.R., 80
lecture method, 87, 118–26
Lewin, K., 72, 73, 119

management theory, 35, 36
mannerisms in tutors, 122, 123
Manpower Services Commission (MSC), 5, 6, 8, 32
Mansbridge, A., 112
McLeish, J., 39
mixed ability groups, 91–104
motivation, 27–38

National Council for Vocational Qualifications (NCVQ), 6, 7, 50
National Extension College (NEC), 143, 144
notetaking, 55, 122, 127
nursing recruitment, 7, 8

objectives, 98–103, 107, 111, 139, 151, 172
Open Business School, 7
Open College, 7, 8, 143, 144, 148, 150
Open College of the Arts, 144
Open learners, 143–57
Open learning materials, 151, 152
Open Tech, 8
Open University (OU), 7, 8, 30, 33, 59, 143, 145, 146, 148, 157
Osler, W., 17
Owen, R., 4

pace in learning, 45
participation, 189–92
Paterson, R.W.K., 175, 180, 181
performance criteria, 101
Powell, M., 19
practice, 51
primary school methods, 97, 98
problem solving in groups, 74, 75
professional education, 6, 7, 50
project method, 158–73

prospectus, 94

radio, local, 164
rapid reading techniques, 55
reception services, 107
reinforcement, 51, 52
relevance, 48, 49, 50
Rogers, C., 12
role play, *see* case study
room arrangement, 83–6
Rosten, L., 109, 110

Save a Life (television series), 50, 51
Schools Council, 182, 183
short term memory, 40, 41, 119
Silburn, R., 159, 164, 165
simulation, *see* case study
Smith, E., 31
social class, 19, 20, 21
Stenhouse, L., 183
Stuart Mill, J., 193, 194

talking too much, 79, 80
Teaching Adults (television series), 4
time pressure in learning, 45
trade union teaching, 4, 146
Training Agency, 5, 8
tutors
  influence, 70
  isolation, 149
  personality, 88, 89
  role, 14, 153, 154, 193
  skills in project leadership, 168, 169

University of Nottingham, 159

vocational education, 5, 7

WEA, 112, 160, 163, 169
Weight Watchers, 74
Welford, A.T., 16
women returners, 34, 35
working class and education, 5, 19–22